Behavior and awareness

Behavior and awareness

A symposium of research and interpretation

Edited by Charles W. Eriksen

Contributors: Charles W. Eriksen

Gregory A. Kimble

Ernest R. Hilgard

Charles D. Spielberger

Don E. Dulany, Jr.

William S. Verplanck

DUKE UNIVERSITY PRESS / *Durham, N. C.* / 1962

© 1962, Duke University Press
Second printing 1971
L.C.C. card no. 62-15952
I.S.B.N. 0-8223-0053-2
Printed in the United States of America

The issue addressed by the papers of the present symposium is one which has recently become of central concern to investigators in the personality area. Stimulated in part by the desire to find a simple analogue for the therapeutic interaction, and in part by a natural fascination with unconscious processes, many researchers have exploited the operant conditioning paradigm to induce experimental changes in verbal response. As this research has begun to proliferate, and to claim the attention of personality psychologists, it has become more and more pertinent to lay bare the nature of the basic processes involved. It unquestionably is a matter of some consequence, for example, whether social reinforcements, appropriately delivered, can strengthen or shift a subject's response dispositions without that subject's being aware of the contingencies involved.

The authors of the following papers attack this pesky problem with discernment and pursue many of its ramifications. Each is firmly committed to an empirical strategy for achieving progressive clarification, and the experimental tactics embraced by these respective strategies are ingenious and quite evidently fruitful. Those who are preparing to read this symposium should set themselves for a rich repast of evidence and ideas. Though overlapping and mutually supportive evidence brings striking agreement with respect to certain conclusions, there is also ample controversy and honest contention. Certainly, no pat solutions to problems of method or theory are to be found here, but many of the solution pathways (as well as the blind alleys) are clearly marked. I am sure that all the contributors to the symposium share my hope and conviction that the following contributions will open the area of "behavior and awareness" to more, and more enlightened, research efforts, and that the difficulties noted will be accepted as a challenge to further inquiry rather than a stimulus for avoidance.

The present symposium was originally organized and planned

with eventual *Journal* publication in mind.   As an important stage in the preparation of the following papers, C. W. Eriksen arranged a symposium on "Behavior and Awareness" at the September, 1962, meetings of the American Psychological Association.   With the exception of Professor Hilgard's paper, each of the following contributions may be said to have developed out of that public presentation.

Edward E. Jones, *Editor*
Journal of Personality

Contents

Behavior and awareness

Figments, fantasies, and follies: A search for the subconscious mind[1]

Charles W. Eriksen, *University of Illinois*

The past six years have witnessed a marked revival of interest in human awareness and its role and effects upon behavior. While it is difficult to trace the history of ideas one can with some justification attribute the current research interest in this area to the experiment of Greenspoon (1955) on verbal conditioning and to the subception experiment of Lazarus and McCleary (1951). These experiments may have been but a manifestation of the *Zeitgeist* but they seem to have laid down the two main lines of experimentation that subsequent research has followed, the problems of learning without awareness and of discrimination without awareness.

As with research on so many other psychological problems there is an early enthusiasm and corresponding lack of critical interpretation. A consequence is a series of criticisms which suggest that the initial results were attributable to methodological errors and artifacts. We stand at this point in the research on behavior and awareness and it is a major purpose of the present symposium to survey and take stock not only of where we are but where we might go. For it has happened often in the history of psychology that important problem areas are abandoned for long periods of time as a result of criticism. Investigators (particularly Ph.D. candidates whose theses constitute a very large proportion of the research publications in psychology) are frightened off by the criticism and the area is left with many unresolved issues. It is true that the methodological pitfalls are many in this research area and it may well be that psychology is not yet far enough advanced in terms of methodology, techniques, and conceptual structure to tackle problems such as human awareness. But it is my contention that from present evidence such a conclusion would be premature.

[1] The research reported in this paper was supported by Mental Health Grant M-1206 from the National Institutes of Health.

It would be particularly unfortunate to abandon research efforts in this problem area now. There is an urgent need for increased clarification of our concepts of the unconscious with reference to psychopathology. The concept of the unconscious is central to most current formulations of personality dynamics in psychopathology. These concepts have changed little since first enunciated by Freud. At that time they constituted a significant contribution, but in the 40 years that have elapsed little change has occurred, little knowledge has been added. Our concepts of personality dynamics and the unconscious are at the level of a crude naturalistic phase in science rather than detailed and exact specification and understanding of the mechanisms involved. Our increasingly recognized inability to deal with psychopathology, either in terms of clinical understanding or therapeutic practice, suggests the urgent need for improved and more precise concepts.

We are now in a position not only to build upon the recent experimental work but also to explore new territory. We not only have learned many of the methodological difficulties to be avoided but have also gained more precise formulations of problems as well as uncovered new questions or problems to be attacked. As an example I think it has become quite clear that we are able to discard the term "subliminal." Research results in the area of discrimination without awareness and, more importantly, from psychophysics quite convincingly have shown that subliminal stimulation is a meaningless term without precise reference to a number of other variables pertaining to the nature of the situation, the statistical criteria involved, and the operating characteristic of the subject. Future research in this area must proceed along the lines of investigating the functional relationship between signal detectability level and the dependent behavior.

In the present paper I shall present in abbreviated form some recent and current research performed in our laboratory. I hope that it will help to indicate new directions for research on awareness and will not only point out the applicability of many concepts from experimental psychology to this area but will also suggest their fruitfulness.

Learning and awareness

With but few exceptions the recent research on learning without awareness has made use of one or the other of two basic techniques, that introduced by Greenspoon (1955) or that introduced by Taffel (1955). In the Greenspoon technique subjects are given minimal instructions other than being asked to say words. When the subject emits words of a selected class (e.g., plural nouns) he is given a social-approval type of reinforcement such as "umhm" or "good." In the Taffel technique the subject is asked to construct sentences using a list of pronouns provided him. Again a social-approval reinforcement is used when the subject selects certain designated pronouns for the construction of his sentences.

From the evidence presented by Dulany and by Spielberger in this symposium, it seems quite clear that learning or behavior change as a function of these experimental conditions does not occur with either technique in the absence of the subject's ability to verbalize mediational steps that occur between the stimulus conditions and changes in his behavior. Further the results presented by Dulany and Spielberger indicate that these changes are also dependent upon the subject's ability to verbalize an intention or a motivation to change his behavior.

While the Dulany and Spielberger experiments and arguments are quite convincing, the limited range of techniques with which they deal constitutes too small a base to conclude that human adults do not learn without awareness. Both the Greenspoon and the Taffel techniques deal exclusively with verbal behavior and it may well be that a verbal response, tied as it is so closely to our criteria of awareness, is incapable of modification without this modification being represented in awareness.

The Greenspoon technique suffers from an additional defect in that it requires the subject to learn a concept, a relatively difficult concept, without awareness. An indication of the difficulty of the concept of "plural nouns" can be seen from a pilot study we conducted several years ago. We employed the Greenspoon technique but deliberately instructed the subjects that the task was concept formation. That is, they were to figure out why the experimenter said "good." Despite this deliberate set for concept attainment only a small percentage of the subjects were able to arrive at the concept of plural nouns within the time limits that Greenspoon had employed. If with a deliberate set to learn or form concepts the majority of subjects were unable to do so, it would seem that this would be a particularly stringent task for demonstrating learning without awareness.

If human learning without awareness does occur, it would seem most likely to appear in relatively simple learning situations. In casting about for suitable conditions it occurred to us that a likely situation for eliciting learning without awareness would be one where the subject has the opportunity to learn a nonsalient perceptual cue as a guide for his behavior.

There are several reasons why one might expect such tasks to reveal learning without awareness. First, perceptual theories, most notably that of Brunswik (1943), have stressed the sensitivity of the perceptual system to contingencies among cues. Thus such probabilistic cues are basic for the perceptual constancies. A second suggestion is found in the almost classic criticism of experiments on the grounds of an uncontrolled but correlated cue that may have guided the subject's responses. This criticism has been applied devastatingly to ESP experiments where the critics have shown that an uncontrolled cue could have been the basis of the subject's correct responses even though the subject may not have been aware he was utilizing this cue. Since experimenters typically go to considerable lengths to control such extraneous cues to prevent their being used as a basis for correct response, a deliberate use of such cues might be a good bet for demonstrating learning without awareness.

We have completed a series of experiments in our laboratory employing this strategy. In the first study subjects were told that they were to participate in an experiment on unconscious perception. They were further told that they would be shown, one at a time, a list of pleasant and unpleasant words but the exposure of the words would be too rapid for them to ever feel that they had recognized the word. It was explained, however, that we had good reason to believe that while they might not consciously recognize the words they, nonetheless, possessed the capacity to make correct emotional discriminations about them. That is, they might get a feeling whether it was pleasant or unpleasant and this was the judgment they were to make. Following exposure of each stimulus word subject was told to say whether he thought it was pleasant or unpleasant using whatever cues he felt might guide him in his decision. He would be corrected after each decision and was told that while we didn't expect him to be too good at this task at the beginning we did think that after a number of corrected trials he would learn to make this discrimination quite well.

While these are the instructions that were administered to the subjects, the actual experimental arrangements were quite different. Twenty two-syllable nonsense syllables were employed as stimuli. They were replicated once with the replication being identical to the original list of 20 with the exception that in the replicated syllables either the first or the last letter had been deleted and replaced by a dash. For half of the subjects the exposure of these altered nonsense syllables was called pleasant, for the other half unpleasant.

A subject's detection function for tachistoscopic exposures was determined during the first ten minutes of the experiment by presenting in random order the letter A or T and requiring the subject to make a forced choice decision as to which letter had been presented. The exposure speed for the nonsense syllables was then selected as the level at which the subject had correctly identified 75 per cent of the presentations of A and T. Subjects were then given 200 presentations of the nonsense syllables, half of the altered type, with knowledge of results after every judgment.

Previous research (Kriekhaus & Eriksen, 1960) had demonstrated the difficulties in verbal-learning experiments of trying to interrogate undergraduate students concerning their awareness. An advantage of the present task was that it permitted a careful and unambiguous list of questions for assessing awareness. At the conclusion of the learning trials we asked the subjects, "You became fairly good at this task. Could you tell me what kind of a cue or what the basis of your judgment was? Did you just have a feeling about it or did the words look different or what?" If the subject did not spontaneously verbalize the correct cue at this point he was asked, "Actually there was a cue present, some basis by which you could tell whether there was a pleasant or an unpleasant word presented—something about the way it looked. Did you notice what this cue was?" If subjects failed to verbalize the correct cue at this point they were told the nature of the cue and asked whether it had been associated with the pleasant or the unpleasant category. These questions enabled us to get around the ambiguity that typically characterizes interrogation for awareness and at the same time, by working down to a forced-choice guess, permitted a more explicit statement of the subject's level of awareness.

The results of this experiment revealed that approximately 33 per cent of the subjects reached the criterion of learning. But examination of their interrogation revealed that all were aware of the presence of the cue. Twenty per cent of the subjects following the first question spontaneously verbalized that there was generally a dash in the front or back of the unpleasant (pleasant) stimuli or that the unpleasant (pleasant) stimuli seemed shorter. The remaining subjects who learned were able to point out the presence of the correct cue in response to the second question.

Sixty-seven per cent of the subjects demonstrated no learning on the task. None achieved the individual criterion of learning nor was the learning curve for the group a significant or actual departure from the chance level. In other words, learning to use the perceptual cue in classification of the stimuli was found only among those subjects who could readily verbalize the presence and nature of the cue. Two of the nonlearning subjects were also able to verbalize the cue although they stated they had not used it.

While these results were completely negative it is possible that the circumstances of the experiment, the set of the subjects, and other undetected factors may have prevented the subjects' learning to use perceptual cues without awareness. Accordingly a subsequent experiment was carried out based upon a finding reported by Brunswik and Herma (1951). They reported producing weight illusions by ecological associations of color cues with differential weight magnitudes. These color cues produced significant illusory effects in the judgment of weights even though the subjects were supposedly unaware of any relationship between the color and weight magnitude.

Their experiment was successfully repeated by Levin (1952) who reported the additional finding that the illusory effect produced by the color cues was as great in subjects having awareness as it was in subjects who were unaware. Unfortunately neither the Brunswik and Herma nor the Levin study contained the specification of the criteria employed in determining awareness. It is problematical whether they were successful in avoiding the pitfalls of correlated hypotheses and the ambiguity of questioning that has plagued so many studies. Nonetheless the suggestive nature of the results led us to conduct the following study.

Subjects were told that they were participating in an experiment to determine the effect of color upon the apparent length of lines. They were presented with pairs of lines of different color and asked to judge which of the two lines was longer (an equal judgment was not allowed). The four colors, red, yellow, green, and blue were employed and, unknown to the subjects, one color was always associated with the longer of the two lines. In group A whenever a blue line was compared with a line of another color the blue line was longer while in group B the contingent color was yellow.

After completing several hundred judgments of all possible color pairs a series of test trials was interspersed with the judgments in which the contingent color was matched with the other colors but both lines were of identical length. If the subjects had learned the ecological association of blue (yellow) with line length, then when confronted with a blue (yellow) line and an equal length line of another color they should tend to choose as longer the blue (yellow) line.

Again it was possible to devise questions that contained minimum ambiguity and yet at the same time were capable of assessing awareness without leading the subject into awareness. Subjects were first asked, "When the judgment was difficult how did you go about making your decision as to which line was longer? Was there any cue or particular characteristic that determined or helped your decision?" Subjects who failed to verbalize the cue in response to this question were then asked, "Did you have the impression that any one of the four colors was more apt to be associated with the longer of the two lines?" If the cue was not verbalized at this point a forced-choice question was asked. "If I told you that one color tended to be associated with the longer of the two lines, what color do you think it would be?"

In analyzing the data it was found that only those subjects (about 25 per cent) who answered the first question in the affirmative and who also indicated that they used the color cue at least occasionally on the difficult discriminations showed any illusory effect on the test trials. The remaining subjects, including those who named the correct color on the forced-choice question, showed no significant nor appreciable illusory effect.

The failure to obtain learning without awareness in this experiment does not seem to be attributable to the fact that the task was not sensitive enough to detect the phenomena. With only about 25 per cent of the subjects becoming aware, it would seem there is ample opportunity for unaware learning to have occurred. The failure to obtain the phenomena taken in conjunction with the negative results of the preceding study suggests that if learning to use perceptual cues without awareness does occur, it is not a very prominent phenomenon in tasks such as we have employed.

We have also attempted to produce learning without awareness in another situation (Paul, Eriksen, & Humphreys, 1962). Most of the work on operant conditioning in human subjects has dealt with verbal behavior and has used as reinforcement various signs of social approval. In pilot work we have discovered a method of administering primary positive reinforcement to human subjects that is comparable to the type of reinforcement employed in animal experimentation. Placing subjects in a heat–humidity chamber with temperature of 105° F. and humidity of 85 per cent we have found that a 10 sec. draft of cool air is a very effective reinforcer. Using this situation we have attempted to bring various nonverbal responses under stimulus control.

Subjects while engaged in a pseudo task in a heat–humidity chamber were given cool air reinforcement for a specific motor response. One group of subjects was reinforced for a face or mouth movement, another group for a hand movement, and a third group for a foot movement. We were successful in obtaining operant-conditioning-like effects in these subjects but only in those who at the completion of the experiment were capable of freely verbalizing the relationship between their behavior and the reinforcement or of stating a correlated hypothesis. To us one of the most surprising aspects of this experiment is that approximately half of the subjects could spend 35 minutes during which something as dramatic as the blast of cool air was completely contingent upon their behavior and yet fail to learn or detect the contingency.

The three experiments summarized above, when taken in conjunction with the evaluation of verbal conditioning offered by Dulany and by Spielberger, are quite discouraging concerning any learning-without-awareness effect.   Since these experiments do not represent a comprehensive survey of the various types of learning tasks, it is of course premature to state that human adults do not learn without awareness.   However, the tasks that have now been investigated do constitute a fair sampling of the learning situations for humans.   The evidence includes concept formation, simple verbal habits, perceptual cue learning, and operant conditioning of nonverbal motor responses.   In none of these situations is impressive or unequivocal evidence of learning without awareness obtained.   It may well be, as I have suggested elsewhere (Eriksen, 1960), that the function of an awareness process in an organism is to detect or be sensitive to important events in the environment. Conditions producing learning represent biological value to the organism and thus do not go undetected by the awareness system. Perhaps another way of stating this is that, other things being equal, we learn what we attend to and attention is inextricably interwoven with our present concepts of awareness.

Incidental stimulation

A recent trend in the research on human awareness has employed a technique that George Klein terms incidental stimulation. While the learning-without-awareness studies have been concerned with the subject's acquisition of responses, the incidental approach uses cues or stimuli whose meaning or sign value is already known to the subjects.   These stimuli are presented in such a form that the subject is unable to report their presence.   Then the effect of these undetected stimuli is looked for in various aspects of subsequent behavior.   Klein and his co-workers have been particularly ingenious in devising techniques for presenting incidental stimulation and for methods of assessing the possible effects (Klein, Spence, Holt, & Gourevitch, 1958; Pine, 1960).

Hilgard, in his symposium paper, has classified a number of the techniques or ways in which a stimulus can be incidentally presented and has discussed various ways in which its presence or effects can be assessed.   Typically, one looks for the effects of incidental stimuli not in a direct manifestation of the stimulus itself but in a subtle or disguised form.   This indirect manifestation has been suggested by the psychoanalytic concept of the primary process.   It is assumed that these incidental stimuli are available to the unconscious mind and to the conscious mind only through the process of condensation, substitution, or distortion that characterizes primary process thinking. Because of this indirect nature of the effects of the stimulation, many possible artifacts can occur (Johnson & Eriksen, 1961). Hilgard provides an illuminating discussion on the problems in trying to determine whether the effects of these incidental stimuli are real or are instead the result of many subtle artifacts.

The various methods used in rendering stimuli incidental, if systematically studied, would tell us much about the nature of awareness or attention, but this so far has not been the central interest of these studies. One of the methods employed is to present the stimulus at such a low energy level that the subject would have a low probability of detecting it. The subject may be directed to try and observe the stimulus or, in other instances, his attention may be engaged on another task. The effects of this incidental stimulation are then sought in autonomic indicators, subsequent response biasing, or themes used in fantasy productions. The stimulus intensity employed varies depending upon the characteristics of the unconscious that are being inferred or tested. At one extreme stimuli are presented at intensities too low to elicit an above-chance discriminated verbal report. Experiments of this kind are attempting to demonstrate what we might call superdiscriminating powers in the unconscious. That is to say, they are attempting to show that levels of discrimination exist below those capable of conscious (verbal) differentiation.

The kind of model or physiological process supposedly underlying such capacities is based upon the somewhat plausible theorizing that stimulus energies impinging upon a sense organ may be too weak to elicit firing all the way to the cortical centers where definitive perception is assumed to occur. However, this low-intensity stimulation may be sufficient to produce effects as far up in the nervous system as the colliculus, in the case of vision, or the geniculate bodies. Now if some effector systems are connected to these lower centers it then becomes possible, theoretically, for discrimination to occur in the absence of awareness (provided awareness is equated with higher neural centers).[2]

[2] It is generally overlooked that discrimination requires not only a sensitivity to differential sensory input, but also enough response differentiation to reflect

Elsewhere (Eriksen, 1960) I have summarized and examined the experimental literature supposedly substantiating such characteristics of unconscious processes and have concluded that at present there is no suggestive nor convincing evidence of such unconscious discriminative powers. I subsequently have encountered no new evidence which would modify this conclusion. In other words, when modern psychophysical procedures are used, no response has turned out to be a more sensitive indicator of perception than the verbal response.

But one need not posit a superdiscriminating unconscious in order to conceive of ways in which low-intensity stimulation may have unconscious effects. While stimulus energies may be too weak to result in awareness or to yield discrimination by any other indicator response, nonetheless, they may leave residual effects in the nervous system which will be revealed in some way in subsequent behavior. This may occur in terms of a lowering of the threshold for the response on succeeding occasions, a biasing of guessing behavior, the selection of fantasy themes, or in other indirect ways.

The microgenetic school of perception has provided a temporal or developmental model of perception in which stimulation passes through successive stages in time before resulting in the completed percept. While much of the experimental work of this school is vitiated by the assumption that time of tachistoscopic exposure bears some monotonic relationship to this developmental process in perception, nevertheless, the conception of perceptual process as proceeding temporally through various stages has some supporting evidence and a certain plausibility.

One might conceive of perception as a series of successive categorizing processes where stimulation is initially broken down into, perhaps, figure-ground and then is successively placed into finer and finer categories by a bracketing-in process until final categorization (recognition) occurs. Such a bracketing-in process of perceptual development is implied by Osgood (1957) when he hypothesizes

---

the differential effects which the sensory side of the process can reflect. In other words, there can be no discrimination unless there are effector paths or responses capable of reflecting variations in the sensory input. While it is possible that response systems may be wired in at lower way stations in sensory systems, these response systems would have to be quite complex in order to make more than just the grossest of discriminations.

that affective evaluation occurs early in the perceptual process, and also by Lazarus (1956) when he speaks of the possibility that a gross type of discrimination, as between threat and nonthreat, may occur early in perceptual development.

Here for both of these investigators the assumption is not only made that perception proceeds by this bracketing-in process but also that the coding system in perception is based upon emotional or meaning aspects of the stimulation rather than physical character-istics or dimensions.

The evidence for such a perceptual model, particularly with reference to the last assumption, is not very positive. Experiments by Eriksen, Azuma, and Hicks (1959), Weiner and Schiller (1960), and Fuhrer and Eriksen (1960) have not only failed to yield evidence of an emotional or affective discrimination occurring prior to specific identification, but instead have indicated that if a bracketing-in type process occurs developmentally in perception, it is most likely organized around physical dimensions of the stimuli rather than meaning or affective ones. Even the work of the microgenetic school suggests that the developmental stages in per-ception are geared around the physical rather than psychological or meaning dimensions.

There is another model that can be invoked to account for effects of low-intensity undetected stimulation upon subsequent behavior. This model also does not require or assume a superdis-criminative unconscious process but does provide for general or gross effects of low-intensity stimulation upon subsequent behavior. This model is borrowed from concepts in the field of behavior theory that center around the idea of the response-evocation thresh-old. In Hullian theory the concept of the effective reaction po-tential recognizes that it is possible for stimulation to be too weak to elicit a response and it is a simple extension to say that below this response evocation threshold stimulation could have had graded effects. Thus the stimulation may have just missed evoking a response or it may have been so weak that the response was no-where near the evocation threshold. It would appear possible that in terms of subsequent responses or on further stimulation it may make a difference whether the first stimulation barely missed evok-ing a response or was so weak that the response was nowhere close to the evocation point.

Behavior theory also provides concepts for the effects of this low-level stimulation that does not evoke a detection response. The concept of gradual strengthening of habits or responses through repeated trials implies that even though a correct response does not occur on a given trial there has been, nonetheless, a gradual incremental strengthening of this response. The current controversy on one-trial learning centers around a concept of this type.

Extension of these concepts to perceptual-recognition behavior and incidental stimulation provides a basis whereby the effects of undetected stimulation upon subsequent behavior can be expected and described. In so doing we also gain a degree of conceptual continuity between research techniques employing incidental stimulation and the traditional research on memory phenomena. Low-intensity stimulation or incidental stimulation that is unreported may be conceived to leave the same trace effects that are implied in the incremental strengthening of responses through repeated trials and the nonspecific or indirect manifestations of incidental stimulation may be capable of discription in terms of known memory distortions (Bartlett, 1932).

The effects of prior experience that are not detectable through recall, or even through recognition, measures are known to be detectable in savings scores when relearning is investigated. Memory also may be quite nonspecific, schematized, or skeletonized, with the specific details having dropped out. In this respect the process and the phenomena would appear quite similar to many of the effects that Hilgard (1958), Goldstein and Barthol (1960), Pine (1960), and Shevrin and Luborsky (1958) have reported in their research on the effects of incidental stimulation upon fantasy and similar productions.

In some of these studies the subjects are presented with brief exposures of complex pictures or scenes and then the effects of unreported objects from the picture are sought in fantasy productions, word associations, or guessing behavior. Most typically the evidence does not show these unreported objects as appearing in direct or specific ways. Instead the effect tends to be predominantly in terms of a biasing for certain categories of response or in terms of general nonspecific contextual similarities.

Resemblance of these effects to observed memory characteristics is quite striking. We are all aware of such effects in our own

memory. We may be unable to recall a person's name but we
have a feeling it begins with a certain letter or that it is a short
name or a long name. Similarly, in remembering faces we may
not be able to precisely locate the situation in which the person
previously has been known, but we have a narrowed-down range
of possible situations in which the prior experience could have
occurred.

The similarity between the incidental-stimulation studies and
the traditional work on human memory is not only in terms of the
applicability of the same concepts but also in terms of methodology.
In experiments such as those of Shevrin and Luborsky and of
Hilgard the complex stimulation is presented to the subject at a
brief tachistoscopic exposure. Recall attempts are required of the
subject and then behavior such as fantasy, dreams, and word association are examined for the effects of the stimulus elements that
were not reported in deliberate recall. The results obtained by
these investigators are quite likely the same as if they had exposed
the picture to the subjects for a minute or longer. But if they had
done so we would have been dealing with the traditional experiment in immediate memory. It is doubtful whether the tachistoscopic exposures are really necessary for obtaining the effects reported by these investigators. It seems likely that other than giving
the experiments the aura of unconscious perception, the tachistoscopic durations only contribute to the usual immediate-memory
techniques by reducing the amount of direct recall.

Viewed in this context the techniques used for recovering or
detecting the missing elements in the picture would not be viewed
as psychoanalytically oriented techniques to get at the primary
process but rather memory measures that are designed to fill in the
tremendous gap between recognition memory scores and savings
scores as traditionally employed.

There are some distinct advantages in looking at the incidental
stimulation phenomena from the point of view of human memory
rather than from the point of view of the psychoanalytic primary-
process concept. This latter concept with its animistic implications and its surplus meanings tends to result in overgeneralization
and overinterpretation of results. In discussing results of experiments of this kind within the context of the primary-process concept, it is very easy either implicitly or explicitly to slip into a

position where one assumes that the specific knowledge of the true stimulus is somewhere buried in the unconscious but is allowed to appear only in distorted form. It is to be noted that a critical evaluation of evidence obtained does not justify the assumption that the true knowledge exists anywhere in the nervous system. Since any results that are obtained in these experiments show the effect of the incidental stimulation only in nonspecific or fragmentary forms, there is no basis for an assumption that these incidental stimuli have left any more than fragmentary traces in the nervous system.[3]

Some current results on incidental stimulation

In recent and current research in our laboratory we have been investigating incidental stimulation at several different levels. At one level we are currently engaged in a systematic examination of the effect of stimulation at different psychophysically determined detectability levels upon a dependent response. Here we are involved in a modernization of the older work of Bressler (1931), Titchner and Pyle (1907), and Dunlap (1900) on the Muller-Lyer illusion. To avoid the arguments over whether the directional arrows that produce the illusion are or are not above or below some ambiguous threshold, we determine the extent of the illusory effect as a function of the detectability level of the directional arrows. The detectability levels for these illusion-producing arrows are determined for individual subjects by presenting the arrows at different intensity levels at the ends of the lines and requiring forced-choice judgments from the subjects not only as to which lines have the arrows but also a judgment as to the directional orientation.

From these data we are able to select illumination levels for the arrows that vary from a chance level to a 100 per cent detectability. These detectability data are then used in presenting the illusion judgments to new samples of subjects. While we have completed only pilot data so far, the results do suggest that the percentage of subjects reporting the illusion is appreciably less than the percentage detectability of the arrows above chance level. This result would be consistent with the interpretation that the

[3] I am indebted to Professor W. C. Becker for pointing out that above criticisms of Freud's primary process concept are quite similar to the criticisms made by Piaget (1951).

arrows have an effect on the apparent length of the lines only if the subject happens to detect them on that particular trial.

Whether or not this result is substantiated by further experimentation, this experiment will give us a functional relationship between the signal-detectability level of stimulation and its illusion-producing effects. In future experiments we hope to apply this technique to studies on size and shape constancy where the various cues on which these constancies depend are varied in detectability level.

A somewhat different approach to incidental stimulation has been carried out in our laboratory by Tatro (1961). Subjects were presented with a picture containing a hidden form or figure. In one of the experimental pictures a campus scene contained a hidden skull formed by the composition of trees and a group of students. In the second experimental picture a beach scene contained a hidden rat formed by a constellation of clouds and shrubbery in the background. Pretesting of these two pictures indicated that approximately 50 per cent of an undergraduate sample spontaneously saw the hidden forms within a two-minute inspection period. Control pictures were devised identical to the experimentals except for slight modifications which destroyed the configuration of the hidden objects.

Four basic groups of subjects were run in the experiment. Group I was shown the picture containing the hidden skull, Group II the picture containing the hidden rat, Group III the control picture for the skull, and Group IV the control picture for the rat. Following exposures to these pictures the subjects were given a series of skeletonized words (words that had been impoverished by systematically deleting parts of the letters yielding an effect somewhat similar to Street Gestalts) and were instructed to try and guess what the original words had been. These skeletonized words had been previously standardized on another sample of subjects so that the approximate proportion of skull- and rat-related completions was known.

Tatro's experiment was guided by the assumption that the subjects exposed to the hidden figure but who failed to find it would contain a proportion of subjects in whom the perception of the hidden figure was just below the evocation threshold. For the control subjects such a perceptual response could be assumed to be appreciably further from the level of evocation. Now if a stimulation which almost results in the evocation of the response leaves some residual effect on the organism, one might anticipate that this trace would have an effect upon the responses to the skeletonized words. Specifically, it might increase the availability of rat-related responses.

Analysis of the data revealed that subjects who had spontaneously seen the hidden rat gave significantly more rat-related completions to the skeletonized words than did the control group. Subjects who had been exposed to the hidden rat picture but who failed to detect it also gave significantly ($p = .05$) more rat-related completions than did the control group but less than the group who had detected the hidden figure.

For the skull picture the results were negative. There were no significant nor appreciable differences between subjects who had or had not detected the hidden skull and the control subjects. In fact the subjects who spontaneously saw the skull had fewer skull-related word completions than did the control subjects. Now one does not have to be a particularly skilled clinician to observe that the failure to obtain results with the skull picture may have been due to the anxiety-evoking nature of a skull. So the experiment was repeated with a larger sample of subjects using only the rat picture. But unfortunately this repetition added only to the ambiguity of the effect. Those subjects who spontaneously detected the hidden rat again showed significantly greater rat-related word completions than did the control group but now Tatro failed to obtain significant effects for those subjects who had been exposed to the hidden rat but failed to detect it. The results were somewhat suggestive, though, in that the mean performance for these latter subjects was more comparable to the performance of the subjects who detected the figure than it was to the control group. Further experimentation on tasks of this kind is definitely needed, but the present results do indicate that if these effects occur they are not very pronounced.

In a third study we have attacked the problem of incidental stimulation at a more molecular and what at first glance might seem a more simple level. If low-intensity stimulation that is undetected by verbal report does have an influence upon subsequent behavior it would seem that a likely place to look for these effects would be in the detectability of subsequent repetitions of the stimulus. Phrasing this in more experimental terms, if a low-energy stimulus is presented twice is there a greater probability of its detection than if presented only once? And if so, what is the optimum time separation between successive presentations of the stimulus or the signal?

We can view this problem as one of central summation. If the first signal is undetected and the second signal occurs within a critical time duration, it may summate with the first so as to yield a detectable signal. The existence of such an effect will be revealed in the increased probability of detection of the second signal as a function of the time lag between its occurrence and that of the first signal. If low-energy signals that are unreported do leave some residual trace or effect in the nervous system, it would seem that this simple method should demonstrate the effect.[4]

In this experiment we used a three-field tachistoscope which provided for independent control of the duration of each of the three fields as well as control of the time period between fields. The stimuli were the capital letters A, T, and U. In the experimental procedure the first session was devoted to obtaining a forced-choice recognition threshold for the individual subjects. This was obtained by presenting an adaptation field followed by a single exposure field and the subject was required to report which one of the three letters had been presented. Following this session fields II and III were set for the duration level where the subject's detection was approximately 50 per cent (about 17 per cent better than chance) while field I was used as an adaptation field. Fields II and III were used to present either a single presentation of one of the letters or a double presentation where the same letter appeared in both fields. The lag time between the cessation of field II and the onset of field III was systematically varied over the three intervals of 0, 5, and 240 ms. lag. Three patterns of stimulation were used: signal presented in field II; signal presented in field III; and same signal presented in both fields II and III. These combinations of stimulation were used for each of the three letters and in every case the subject made a forced judg-

---

[4] It is possible that a prior but undetected signal may have an inhibitory effect upon a subsequent signal that occurs at certain time lags.

ment.   To prevent retinal summation the stimuli were varied randomly around the fixation point.

By comparing the probability of detection for double stimulation with that of a single stimulation we can assess whether or not an undetected stimulation has a facilitory (inhibitory) effect.   It is to be noted, however, that a higher level of detection for the double stimulation will not automatically indicate that the first stimulation facilitated the second stimulation.   It is necessary to make an allowance for the fact that with the double stimulation the subject has two chances to detect the signal.

The receptor-perceptual system contains a certain amount of random noise.   If a burst of noise should occur at the same time as the occurrence of one signal it might interfere with detection, but the noise may have subsided by the occurrence of the second signal.   Depending upon the distribution of this noise envelope in time, we would expect a certain time lag to yield noncorrelation between errors in the system.   In the case where the time lag is such as to result in noncorrelated noise and the detectability of single stimulations is 50 per cent, we would expect the probability of detection of one or the other signal to be 75 per cent.   For if the probability of detection of the first signal is 50 per cent and the probability of detection of the second signal is 50 per cent, in the case of lack of correlation of errors the second signal should be detected on 50 per cent of the errors of the first signal.   This would result in an over-all detectability level of 75 per cent.   If undetected signals have a residual effect in the nervous system so as to facilitate subsequent signals, then for double stimulation a significant rise in detectability level over 75 per cent should be found at some time lag between the two signals.

Fifteen subjects were run at each of the time lags.   The results of this study are shown in Figure 1.   In examining the data in this figure, we note that there is little or no indication of any residual effects of an undetected stimulation upon the detectability of a subsequent signal.   For the time lags studied there is no case where a detectability for the double stimulation approaches the value of 75 per cent.

But there are many other things that are revealed in this figure.   It can be seen that what at first seemed to be a rather simple way of determining whether or not undetected stimulation leaves

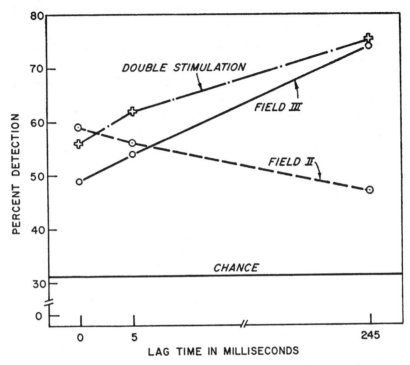

Figure 1. Detection as a function of exposure field and lag time between first and second signals.

residual effects in the nervous system has actually involved us in some rather complex problems concerning the perceptual process. Some of the more interesting aspects of this experiment are reflected in what happens to a single stimulation depending upon whether it is preceded or followed by a blank field where only light is presented. The curve for single stimulation preceded by a light shows a gain in detectability over the three lag times whereas the condition where the signal is presented first and is then followed by the blank field of light results in progressive loss in detectability over lag times.

This is not the place to speculate on the mechanisms that may be responsible for these characteristics but these results make a point. When we are building concepts at the level of personality theory it would seem wise not to ignore what is known about the receptor-perceptual mechanisms upon which these concepts occasionally rest. Hebb (1949) has argued forcefully that psychologists should utilize the current facts of brain neurology and physiology when they are building constructs and models that presuppose certain neural-physiological processes. A similar plea can be made to personality and clinical psychologists that when building their theories they should not ignore what is known concerning basic physiological and perceptual characteristics.

Some general considerations

While the studies I have summarized have not been particularly successful in demonstrating behavior without awareness, they do suggest some of the breadth of the possible experimental approaches to this problem area as well as some of the commonalities between research in this area and general experimental psychology. There are many other facets of behavior and awareness, though, that have received little or no experimental attention. The research on learning without awareness has brought to the fore again the old problem of the role of verbalization in the control and specificity of behavior. Dulany in his symposium paper presents a very promising framework for re-examining the problems on the role of verbalization in behavior and for investigation of the degree of correlation between verbal and nonverbal behavior.

Another problem needing experimental attention is performance without awareness. While we have been unsuccessful as yet in unequivocally demonstrating learning without awareness, there seems little doubt that performance without awareness occurs and occurs frequently. The evidence for this phenomena is predominantly introspective, but it is so strong that most of us are convinced that it is real. A broad-scale attack on the problem of awareness should include experimental studies not only of how overlearned perceptual-motor responses become automatic, but also should orient itself toward investigating ways and techniques by which behavior that has become automatic is brought back into awareness.

I suspect the problems concerning overlearned automatic behavior have been neglected in the laboratory because of the considerable time expenditure required to produce the appropriate degree of overlearning. However, one can study behavior that has been overlearned on the subject's own time, so to speak. Most subjects have already acquired the perceptual motor skills involved in automobile driving. By employing experimental tasks in which a high degree of positive transfer of these skills can be obtained, the experimental time per subject should be capable of reduction to a feasible period. And of course the large pool of introductory psychology students available for subjects must include a large number who have mannerisms or habits which are susceptible to experimental manipulation.

Another aspect of awareness that requires experimental attention concerns the subject's subjective confidence. In judgmental tasks requiring difficult discriminations it is not uncommon to find that subjects can make above-chance discriminations or show above-chance accuracy although they report a subjective feeling of "pure" guessing. In preliminary work in our laboratory we have found marked individual differences in what we have termed the subjective confidence interval. We have measured this interval by taking the difference between a forced-choice discrimination threshold for a subject and a free report threshold where he assigns a confidence level to his judgment. For some subjects these two points are virtually identical whereas for other subjects there is a wide range between the point where the discrimination curve deviates from chance at the forced choice level and the point where the subject reports confidence in his judgments.

Aside from the possible relevance of these individual differences to other personality variables, the subjective confidence interval would seem to provide an opening wedge for studying the subjective aspects of awareness. The subjective confidence interval is quite comparable to the concept of the response operating characteristic described by Egan (1958) and many of the methods that Egan among others have used in examining or investigating the parameters of the ROC are relevant to describing or understanding this subjective aspect of awareness.

Finally we should take cognizance of the fact that in dealing with these problems of awareness we are also dealing with the question of attention. Recent interest in problems of attention and immediate memory traces by experimental psychology should not be overlooked as we approach this problem area with our personality orientation. Research on incidental stimulation can be expected not only to increase our understanding of fantasy and other irrational human behavior but concurrently can be expected to yield information about the attending process in the human subject. An adequate model of attention can be expected to encompass most, if not all, of the phenomena with which we are concerned in this research area.

References

Bartlett, F. C. *Remembering.* Cambridge, England: Cambridge Univer. Press, 1932.

Bressler, J. Illusion in the case of subliminal visual stimulation. *J. gen. Psychol.,* 1931, 5, 244-250.

Brunswik, E. Organismic achievement and environmental probability. *Psychol. Rev.,* 1943, 50, 255-272.

Brunswik, E., & Herma, H. Probability learning of perceptual cues in the establishment of a weight illusion. *J. exp. Psychol.,* 1951, 41, 281-290.

Dunlap, K. Effect of imperceptible shadows on the judgments of distance. *Psychol. Rev.,* 1900, 7, 435-453.

Egan, J. P. Recognition memory and the operating characteristic. Technical Note, Contract No. AF 19(604)-1962, 15 June 1958.

Eriksen, C. W. Discrimination and learning without awareness: A methodological survey and evaluation. *Psychol. Rev.,* 1960, 67, 279-300.

Eriksen, C. W., Azuma, H., & Hicks, Rosalie B. Verbal discrimination of pleasant and unpleasant stimuli prior to specific identification. *J. abnorm. soc. Psychol.* 1959, 59, 114-119.

Fuhrer, M., & Eriksen, C. W. The unconscious perception of the meaning of verbal stimuli. *J. abnorm. soc. Psychol.,* 1960, 61, 432-439.

Goldstein, J. J., & Barthol, R. P. Fantasy responses to subliminal stimuli. *J. abnorm. soc. Psychol.,* 1960, 60, 22-26.

Greenspoon, J. The reinforcing effect of two spoken sounds on the frequency of two responses. *Amer. J. Psychol.,* 1955, 68, 409-416.

Hebb, D. O. *The organization of behavior.* New York: Wiley & Sons, 1949.

Hilgard, E. R. *Unconscious processes and man's rationality.* Urbana, Ill.: Univer. Illinois Press, 1958.

Johnson, H., & Eriksen, C. W. Preconscious perception: A re-examination of the Poetzl phenomenon. *J. abnorm. soc. Psychol.,* 1961, 62, 497-503.

Klein, G. S., Spence, D. P., Holt, R. R., & Gourevitch, Susannah. Cognition without awareness: Subliminal influences upon conscious thought. *J. abnorm. soc. Psychol.,* 1958, 57, 255-266.

Krieckhaus, E. E., & Eriksen, C. W. A study of awareness and its effects on learning and generalization. *J. Pers.,* 1960, 28, 503-517.

Lazarus, R. S. Subception: Fact or artifact? A reply to Eriksen. *Psychol. Rev.,* 1956, 63, 343-347.

Lazarus, R. S., & McCleary, R. A. Autonomic discrimination without awareness: A study of subception. *Psychol. Rev.,* 1951, 58, 113-122.

Levin, M. M. Inconsistent cues in the establishment of a weight illusion. *Amer. J. Psychol.,* 1952, 65, 517-532.

Osgood, C. E. Motivational dynamics of language behavior. In M. R.

Jones (Ed.), *Nebraska symposium on motivation:* Univer. Nebraska Press, 1957.

Paul, G., Eriksen, C. W., & Humphreys, L. G.   Use of temperature stress with cool air reinforcement for human operant conditioning.   *J. exp. Psychol.,* (in press).

Piaget, J.   *Play, dreams and imitation in childhood.*   New York: Norton, 1951.

Pine, F.   Incidental stimulation: A study of preconscious transformation. *J. abnorm. soc. Psychol.,* 1960, 60, 68-75.

Shevrin, H., & Luborsky, L.   The measurement of preconscious perception in dreams and images: An investigation of the Poetzl phenomena. *J. abnorm. soc. Phychol.,* 1958, 56, 285-294.

Taffel, C.   Anxiety and the conditioning of verbal behavior.   *J. abnorm. soc. Psychol.,* 1955, 51, 496-501.

Tatro, D.   The effect of an undetected hidden figure on subsequent responses.   Unpublished master's dissertation, Univer. of Illinois, 1961.

Titchner, E. B., & Pyle, W. H.   The effect of imperceptible shadows on the judgment of distance.   *Proc. Amer. Phil. Soc.,* 1907, 46, 94-109.

Weiner, M., & Schiller, P. H.   Subliminal perception or perception of partial cues.   *J. abnorm. soc. Psychol.,* 1960, 61, 124-137.

Classical conditioning and the problem of awareness

Gregory A. Kimble, *Duke University*[1]

Although I intend to honor my assignment in this symposium and to deal in the main with the problem of awareness as it relates to classical conditioning, I would like to view the topic in broad perspective to bring to your attention certain evidence and lines of argument not ordinarily included in discussions of this topic.

The present-day interest in the relationship between behavior and awareness exists in part because of a suspected connection with the psychoanalytic concepts of conscious and subconscious. Viewed in this light, the tendency is to regard research on this problem as stemming from the work of Freud. My guess, however, is that the credit should go, not to Freud, but to William James, at least with respect to the set of ideas which appear to dominate research in this area today.

As is well known, James was particularly interested in the problem of hysteria. In his *Principles of Psychology* (James, 1890), he devoted a considerable amount of space to the discussion of this form of neurosis, especially to the phenomena of hysterical cutaneous anesthesia. Among others, he described cases of persons who could feel nothing in one hand but exhibited the following remarkable behavior. Seated before a screen, and being instructed to describe whatever appeared there, the patient would be touched two or three times on the anesthetic member. Although he could not feel the touch, the patient reported seeing as many objects of some sort on the screen as there were taps on his hand. Similarly a pencil stroke along the hand might produce a corresponding visual impression on the screen. Today, of course, many of us would be very suspicious of the validity of these reports. There is a sense, however, in which their accuracy is unimportant. For, whether or

[1] The preparation of this paper and the collection of the data presented in Fig. 2 were facilitated by a grant from the National Science Foundation: NSF-G 7079.

not the behavioral facts are correct, James went on to offer a theory to account for such effects in which he developed a distinction between primary and secondary consciousness and even used the word, "sub-conscious," in his discussion. The following quotation summarizes his view neatly.

"This whole phenomenon shows how an idea which remains itself below the threshold of a certain conscious self may occasion associative effects therein. The skin-sensations unfelt by the patient's primary consciousness awaken nevertheless their usual visual associates therein." (James, 1890, Vol. II, p. 205 n.)

A similar idea appears in James's discussion of the mechanism through which discriminative performance profits from training. In this context, James noted that the separate facial features of two individuals whose appearances strike us as very different might really be very similar. That is, if one considered the nose, chin, eyes, and so on, one at a time, these single characteristics might be indistinguishable. Yet, putting the individual features together to produce the two faces leads to the construction of two highly different physiognomies. This suggests that influences which are too small to notice have an effect at some unconscious level, and that these unconscious effects add to produce a suprathreshold total. Again we need not worry about the adequacy of this interpretation. The only point I wish to make is that the idea that effects beneath the threshold of awareness have an influence upon behavior is about as old as psychology itself.

The problem from the point of view of the theorist of learning

In more recent times interest in this general field has tended to focus quite sharply on the question whether *learning* without awareness is possible. Put this generally, the question leads immediately to difficulties. We know, for example, that animals as low in the phylogenetic scale as the earthworm are able to acquire simple habits. Is the worm *aware* as it develops this knowledge or not? Without laboring the point, it seems fairly obvious that there is a serious definitional problem, that of defining awareness, which remains to be solved. Until the solution is achieved, it is possible to do experimental work on the problem by using a limited definition which equates awareness of an event with the ability to verbal-

ize correctly with respect to it. This operational restriction of the
concept seems to have been accepted by most investigators in the
field. It should be recognized, however, that its acceptance places
clear limits on the generality of whatever conclusions may be
reached on the relationship between learning and awareness. Furthermore, it is probably inappropriate even to discuss the matter
in connection with the learning of young children, certain of the
very old, many brain-damaged individuals, and most mental de-
fectives, as well as in the case of lower animals. In each of these
instances, there is reason to doubt the verbal competence of the
organism.

   Thus, even to approach the question, we must restate it, and ask
something like this: Is learning without awareness possible in the
case of human organisms with normal verbal equipment? Let us
begin by taking the question completely literally, and ask, on our
way to an answer, when is an organism completely unaware?
Obviously: When it is dead. And everyone recognizes that, except
perhaps in television's *Twilight Zone,* dead organisms do not learn.
More seriously, perhaps we could agree that, short of death, an
individual is as near as he ever is to a complete lack of awareness
in profoundly deep sleep. This of course leads to the question,
does a person in deep sleep ever learn anything? Here the answer
seems quite clearly to be no, a conclusion to which the results
obtained by Simon and Emmons (1956) lead with considerable
insistence. Using a criterion for depth of sleep based upon characteristics of the electroencephalogram, these investigators found
no dependable evidence for learning in subjects who were deeply
asleep. As has happened in other studies in this general area, however, the distinction between waking (awareness) and sleeping
(lack of awareness) was hard to draw sharply. There were tran-
sition zones between sleep and waking; and in the very lightest
stages of sleep some learning did occur. But such evidence seems
only to support the conclusion that some awareness is necessary
for learning to occur.

   At this point, someone is sure to protest that this isn't exactly
what is meant by the term awareness in discussions of learning
without awareness. If one asks what *is* meant, the forthcoming
answer is likely to be pretty vague; but if one were to derive an
answer from the procedures actually employed by investigators in

the field, he would come to the conclusion that what is involved is the recognition (or lack of it) in subjects who are fully aware of certain features of the experimental situation. Beyond this there seems to be agreement that interest centers on the question whether, for learning to occur, the subject must be aware of a particular relationship: that between the conditioned stimulus (in the case of classical conditioning) or a response (in the case of instrumental learning) and the reinforcer. In effect the question is whether subject must be aware of the relationship which, on other grounds, we know to be necessary for learning to occur.

The particular items selected for examination by investigators in the field do not exhaust the possibilities; and it may be of some interest to put the question more broadly. In the case of classical conditioning, where the major components of the process (conditioned and unconditioned stimuli and responses) are well recognized and easily identified, it may be useful to raise the question in terms of the traditional categories: In order to learn does the organism have to be aware of the UCS, UCR, CS or what? We should recognize at the outset that, asked in this limited way, we are apt to get a limited answer; for it may very well be that the laws of classical conditioning are not the laws of all learning. Therefore, the answer to which we come may not apply generally; but reserving this point for later treatment, let us proceed.

For purposes of this discussion, it will be possible to consider conditioned and unconditioned responses together. Although they are probably never exactly identical in form, they are the same with respect to the characteristic of interest to us here. There seems to be no reason whatsoever to hold that the subject must be aware of the reactions being modified for this form of learning to occur. Indeed, some conditionable responses are ones which the learner typically knows nothing about. These include the Galvanic Skin Response (GSR), pupillary dilation, details of the heart-rate pattern, and certain features of the alpha rhythm of the electro-encephalogram. In either their conditioned or unconditioned form, these responses occur in the complete absence of awareness.

This leaves us with the question of the stimuli involved in conditioning. Does the organism have to be aware of the conditioned and/or unconditioned stimuli for conditioning to occur? In ordinary conditioning studies, these are both conspicuous features of the environment which the subject would be unlikely not to notice. Moreover, evidence from various forms of observing reaction supports the suggestion that lower animals notice the CS as well as the UCS. This does not, however, establish the necessity for the awareness of these conditions; and, if one accepts the recent work of the Russians on interoceptive conditioning, evidence is accumulating that perception by the organism of the conditioned stimulus may *not* be necessary. The second edition of *Hilgard and Marquis' Conditioning and Learning* provides the following illustrative example borrowed from Razran (1961).

> Intestinal loops were isolated surgically, in two dogs, and tubes were provided for the introduction of liquids (to serve as CS's) into the intestine. For one dog the CS was a .2% solution of hydrochloric acid; for the other it was a 5.5% solution of glucose. In each case the UCS was a shock administered to the left hind paw 10 to 15 seconds later. The animal receiving the hydrochloric acid CS formed a stable motor CR in just 16 trials. The animal receiving glucose required 30. The fact that the CS was the specific chemical solution was demonstrated by the ability of the subject to form a discrimination between the liquid used for the CS and a saline solution of the same volume and temperature. [Kimble, 1961, p. 52]

The point of this demonstration, of course, is that there is, so far as we know, no representation in awareness of chemical stimuli influencing the intestine.

Such evidence leads Razran to stress the point that these classically conditioned responses are ones of which we are normally unaware: "Unlike the continuum of exteroceptive stimulation which is the body-material of all our conscious experience, the continuum of interoceptive stimulation leads largely to unconscious reactions." As is apt to be the case with Russian work, which Razran reviewed in reaching his conclusion, it is hard to evaluate the experimental basis for this statement, because no details of procedure or results are available. On the other hand, results like these seem to have been obtained in numerous Russian experiments; so for the moment let us accept Razran's interpretation. In terms of our present discussion, this would be that classical conditioning sometimes occurs in cases where the conditioned stimuli are completely out of awareness.

In the case of the unconditioned stimulus, we find that successful conditioning has probably never been carried out without the use of some form of fairly intense unconditioned stimulus, although it is possible to substitute direct stimulation of the central nervous system for peripheral stimulation. Moreover, there is some evidence that events which attenuate the influence of the UCS (low intensity, previous adaptation trials) interfere with conditioning. Such evidence suggests very strongly that awareness of the UCS is necessary for conditioning to occur. At least tentatively, the data available on classical conditioning seem to support a conclusion which has also been reached by certain investigators in the field of verbal conditioning, that awareness of the reinforcer is the critical factor.

There is, however, one line of evidence which might be interpreted to mean that awareness even of the UCS may not be essential. This evidence is to be found in certain work on perceptual learning, of which that of Professor Ivo Kohler at Innsbruck is the most impressive.[2] As many of you know, Professor Kohler's specialty is that of having his subjects (the chief of whom is usually Professor Kohler) wear spectacles which distort the world in various ways in order to study the accommodation of the subject to such distortion. In one of his experiments, Kohler prepared spectacles with the lenses split down the middle, each half being a different color. In one case, the two left-hand halves were blue and the right-hand halves were a complementary yellow. This arrangement meant that whenever the subject glanced to the left, the world appeared bluish. Whenever he glanced to the right, it appeared yellowish. The subjects wore these spectacles for 60 days.

In order to test the influence of the spectacles upon the perception of color, Kohler devised apparatus in which the subject could, if necessary, add yellow or blue light to an achromatic field in order to make the field appear a neutral gray. That is, if for some reason the visual field appeared yellow, the subject could add blue to neutralize the yellow. Or, if the field appeared blue, he could add yellow for the same purpose.

Tests of this sort were carried out at the very beginning of the experiment and at the end of it. There were four conditions, two without glasses and two with the glasses in place. In each case, some of the tests were made when the field was viewed glancing at it

---

[2] The account which follows relies upon personal conversations with Professor Kohler during a semester he spent at Duke University, a colloquium which he delivered at Duke in the spring of 1959, and a draft of an unpublished paper which he was preparing during the same period.

from the left and some were made when subject glanced at it from the right. The general results of the experiment were these: at the beginning of the study, tested without the glasses, the subjects were able to perceive the neutral gray very accurately and this accuracy was unaffected by the direction of the subjects' view. Tested with the glasses, however, they had to add large amounts of yellow when the field was viewed through the blue half of the lenses. Conversely, when it was viewed through the yellow half of the lenses, they had to add blue. Sixty days later, at the end of the experiment, their performance was very different. Now, with the spectacles in place, the subject had to add much less of the color which was complementary to that through which it was viewed.

Even more impressive were the results with the spectacles removed. Under these conditions, the subject had to add a large amount of yellow or blue (to obtain what they perceived as achromatic) depending upon the direction from which the gray field was viewed. When the gaze was in the direction in which the eyes had looked for 60 days through the blue half of the glasses it was necessary to add blue; when the gaze was from the other direction, it was necessary to add yellow. Thus, for one half of the visual field, it was as if, having worn the blue glasses for a long period of time, the world appeared yellow when the glasses were removed, and blue had to be added to obtain the experience of gray. An exactly complementary effect occurred when the subject glanced at the visual field, without the glasses, but in the direction where he had previously seen the world through yellow lenses.

It is important to stress, in connection with this experiment, that exactly the same retinal areas seem to have responded differently, depending upon the angle of regard. For this reason, Professor Kohler considers this a case of conditioning in which a basic adaptational process becomes associated with the kinesthetic stimulation produced by turning the eyes to the right or left. It seems unlikely, if this is correct, that either CS or UCS was, in the usual sense, a matter of direct awareness. Together with the evidence described earlier in this paper, this suggests that certain forms of classical conditioning may occur under circumstances where none of the features of the conditioning situation is one of which the subject is aware.

On the other hand this modification of behavior occurs under

circumstances which are enough different from those employed in
the usual classical conditioning experiment that one wonders
whether the two types of learning are the same. This is one of
the points to which I had reference in making the suggestion that
the answer to our question obtained from an examination of
classical conditioning might be limited. The trend in present-day
theorizing in the field of learning seems to be toward a multiplica-
tion of the number of recognized forms of learning. One possibility is that it will be found that certain of these occur without
awareness and that for others awareness is a necessity.

Useful distinctions borrowed from the
general psychology of learning

As a preliminary to the development of certain further ideas, I
should like now to turn to some other points which are suggested
by the kind of analysis familiar to the psychologist of learning.
These points involve a set of distinctions which seem to have a
potential clarifying power in connection with the problem of behavior and awareness.

Learning without awareness vs. performance without awareness

The first of these is the distinction between learning and performance. Most theoretical positions in this field make this distinction in one form or another. The general idea is that any bit of
behavior is the product of two sets of factors. One of these is a set
of relatively permanent factors such as traits and habits, or more
generally, capacities; the other is a set of relatively more temporary
processes, the most important of which are motivation, set, and
various forms of inhibition. A given degree of learning may lead
to performances of different strengths, depending upon the momentary values of these temporary factors. Extending this distinction
to the problem of learning without awareness leads to the obvious
thought that it may be important to distinguish performance without awareness from learning without awareness and to recognize
that the two accomplishments are probably not the same.

There seems to be no reason to doubt that many highly
routinized performances do indeed occur completely beyond the

performer's awareness.   To cite just one simple example, when one is driving an automobile and approaches an intersection with the intention of turning to the right, he will note (if he happens to introspect upon his behavior) that there is a strong tendency to look to the left and a much weaker one to look to the right, both of which are automatic and noticed only rarely.   It seems very likely that the predominant tendency to look to the left was established long ago and was based upon the importance of paying greatest attention to the traffic coming from the left, because that is traffic into which one is moving and the source of greatest danger.   In this case, present performance is without awareness although original learning may have been accompanied by acute awareness.   It is not difficult to think of many similar sequences of everyday behavior.   The point, of course, is that performance without awareness does not prove the existence of learning without awareness.

Verbalization of sequence vs. conditioned response

A second distinction, drawn quite strictly from studies of classical conditioning, is the following.   In almost any such experiment the subject is apt to learn two very different things, the sequence of events as they occur on a typical trial and the conditioned response.   In a typical eyelid conditioning experiment, for example, the subject will learn that the air puff, which we call the unconditioned stimulus, occurs a short period following the tone used as a conditioned stimulus.   The usual subject can verbalize this sequence of events after just one or two exposures to it.   The occurrence of a conditioned reaction, however, may not take place until many trials later.   It is quite obvious that the verbalization of the sequences of stimuli and the acquisition of the conditioned response are two very different forms of learning, both of which occur in the conditioning situation.

The question to ask next, of course, is whether the occurrence of one of these kinds of learning always implies the occurrence of the other.   The evidence indicates that the answer to this question is probably no, but the relationships are complex.   In some cases, verbal knowledge of the sequence of stimuli seems to interfere with conditioning.   Razran has routinely found (e.g., 1955) that knowledge of conditioning inhibits the development of conditioned salivary reactions. There are other cases in which about all that can be said is that verbal understanding is no aid to conditioning in cases where one might expect such knowledge to be of value. Examples of this come from certain partial reinforcement experiments in eyelid conditioning in which regularly patterned sequences of reinforced and nonreinforced trials, such as single and double alternation are used. In these experiments (Grant, Riopelle, & Hake, 1950) the subjects leave the experiment perfectly able to tell the experimenter that the air puff occurred, for example, on two trials; then was omitted for two trials; then was reintroduced for two more trials, and so on. The same subjects, however, may have given no conditioned responses at all; and the performance of groups of subjects conditioned with patterned reinforcement is always very inferior to the performance obtained when every trial is reinforced. In this demonstration, awareness is of no value in the establishment of the CR. This fact provides inferential support for the conclusion that awareness, similarly, is probably not the critical thing in the acquisition of the CR under more favorable circumstances.

Having developed the distinction between learning and performance and that between learning and the verbalization of sequences, let us examine their implications for study of learning without awareness, using verbal conditioning as an example. In these studies, the typical result is an increase in the frequency of some verbal response such as the use of the pronouns "I" and "We" or the emission of plural nouns. This result does not prove that the tendency to make these responses is *learned* in the experiment. For, as we have seen, performance changes may not reflect learning, but rather changes in other factors such as motivation or the subject's perception of the requirements of the situation. Thus, it is entirely possible that the changes in question depend upon the subject's learning the contingency at work in the experiment (that is becoming "aware") and that the performance of the reinforced response represents nothing more than the transfer to this situation of responses already available to the subject. In other words, it is not difficult to imagine that such responses as saying "I" and "We" or emitting plural nouns are not learned at all in these experiments. As the subject becomes aware of the rules, he may decide to go along with the obvious little game the experimenter wants to play, or he may not if there seems little point to it.

Beginning with the basic assumptions of the theorist of learning, we thus arrive at an interpretation which suggests that the results in question not only do not occur in the absence of awareness, but also do not involve learning. This interpretation, in the absence of evidence, might either be right or wrong. The evidence, however, as outlined by Dulany and Spielberger in this symposium seems to support such a conclusion. The chief contribution which my analysis of the problem has made is in demonstrating that the likelihood that the evidence would support such a conclusion might have been anticipated on methodological grounds. To summarize the reasons for this very briefly: students of learning recognize as important a distinction between learning and performance which provides for alternative explanations for any learning-like change in behavior. Beginning with this distinction, one is led to look for its application in the studies of learning without awareness. One important possibility, suggested by certain results of classical conditioning experiments, is that the subject learns nothing more in these experiments than the ability to verbalize sequences. Experimental evidence appears to support this suspicion. Since, as we have seen, the ability to verbalize correctly is a rough operational equivalent of awareness, this means that these might better be viewed as experiments on the learning *of* awareness rather than of learning without it.

Reinterpreted in this way, the verbal-conditioning experiments may actually be of greater interest than in their original conception, in that several interesting questions now arise. For example, the whole issue of the nature of awareness, which has received little treatment since the early part of this century, might be reintroduced in an operationally meaningful way as work on verbal conditioning proceeds. If the acquisition of verbal understanding (that is, awareness) is one of the main things which occurs in the usual verbal-conditioning experiment, is this a form of learning which occurs with or without awareness? I know of no data which are relevant to this question; but (taking a lead again from other work on learning) it may be that the situation is like that in eyelid conditioning. In these experiments the typical report is that at the moment of occurrence the subject is unaware of the reaction: immediately thereafter he becomes aware of having made it, although he may not be able to tell whether or not the blink anticipated the air puff. It is possible that a parallel state of affairs exists in connection with the emergence of awareness in verbal conditioning. In any case, the events immediately surrounding the subject's initial awareness of the contingencies in verbal conditioning seem to me to represent a topic which is worthy of investigation.

The effect of verbal processes on classical conditioning

So far we have seen that it is useful to distinguish between the acquisition of the verbal recognition of sequences (awareness) and the acquisition of the conditioned response, and to understand that the former kind of learning does not insure the occurrence of the latter. At least in this sense the two processes are independent of each other. In other ways, however, there is good reason to believe that verbal processes (that is, awareness of contingencies) have a more important influence upon conditioning. Three such effects seem reasonably well established. These are: (a) the effect of set; (b) the mediation of gaps in time; and (c) the mediation of transfer and differentiation. These effects occur, of course, in instrumental learning as well as in classical conditioning. The discussion which follows is limited to classical conditioning for purely practical reasons, involving limitations of space.

The effect of set

There is an item of laboratory lore in the field of eyelid conditioning according to which something like 90 per cent of the effectiveness of the conditioning procedure for individual subjects depends upon events which occur within about 20 sec. of the time subject enters the laboratory, considerably before the beginning of the experiment. These crucial events consist of a set of facilitating or interfering attitudes developed in subject by his initial contact with the experimenter, his reaction to the experimental room, and other incidental features of the situation. The precise figure, 90 per cent, is probably only a modest exaggeration; there is no doubt that matters external to the intentions of the experimenter are important in determining the level of conditioning ultimately attained.

In most laboratories this has led to the development of procedures (previous training of experimenters, instructions to subjects, pre-training trials, etc.) designed to standardize the experimental situation along lines which produce reasonably good conditioning. The number of studies attempting an experimental manipulation of these features of the experiment, especially the influence of such personal characteristics as attitude and set, is unfortunately smaller.

A good example of an experiment in this latter, less popular, category is that of Norris and Grant (1948) who studied the effects of different instructions.   These two investigators compared the rate of conditioning obtained following instructions usually designated as facilitatory and inhibitory.   The results of this experiment together with the essential elements of the instructions appear in Figure 1.   It is quite clear that in this case a verbally established set has an important effect upon conditioning.   Again, however, it is important not to confuse the set, itself, with the effect it has upon learning.

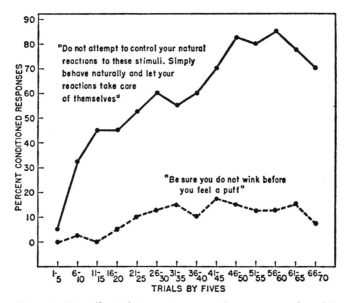

Figure 1. The effect of instructions upon the progress of eyelid conditioning. The main emphases in the two different sets of instructions as suggested by the quotations appearing in the figure. (Norris & Grant, 1948)

The verbal mediation of gaps in time

As an illustration of the way in which verbal factors may serve a time-bridging function, I will describe a preliminary experiment which has since been replicated, but not yet published.[3] It is well known, of course, that one of the most important variables controlling the level of conditioning is the interstimulus interval, that is, the time between conditioned and unconditioned stimuli. An interval in the neighborhood of .5 sec. is nearly optimal; and extending the interval to as much as 1.5 sec. results in a much lower level of conditioning. Parenthetically, it may be important to point out that extending the interval in this manner has little influence upon the ability of the subjects to verbalize the sequence of events in the experiment, but it has a great effect upon the level of conditioning obtainable. This fits in with the previous point about the independence of conditioning and the ability to describe the details of the experimental procedure.

Turning to the point about mediation, however, what would happen if the subject were to utter some verbal response which in some sense filled a portion of the interval between conditioned and unconditioned stimuli? To investigate this question, we compared conditioning at 1.5-sec. intervals with conditioning at a .5-sec. interval, but developed two versions of the 1.5-sec. procedure. One involved the standard method of presenting trials while the subject simply sat passively in the experimental situation. The CS, a dim light, came on, followed in 1.5 sec. by the UCS, an air puff to the cornea. In the other version of the experiment, the subject was instructed to say the word "thousand" when the CS came on. Our reasoning was that it would take the subject about .2 sec. to respond and perhaps another .8 sec. to say the word "thousand." This would mean, then, that the end of the word thousand would occur at approximately the optimal time prior to the unconditioned stimulus. If saying the word thousand were capable of bridging the gap in time, we would expect the level of conditioning with the 1.5-sec. interval under these circumstances to be about the same as that obtained with a .5-sec. interval. This is what happened in the experiment. The results of the study appear in Figure 2.

[3] The replication was by Dr. R. A. King and his students at the University of North Carolina.

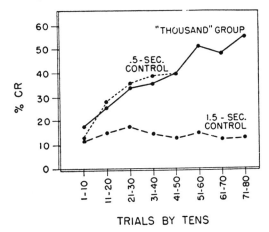

Figure 2. The effect of a verbal mediator upon the progress of eyelid conditioning. The 1.5-sec. control group and the "thousand" group were conditioned with a 1.5-sec. interstimulus interval; but the subjects in the "thousand" group responded to the onset of the CS by saying the word "thousand." The .5-sec. control group was conditioned with a CS-UCS interval of .5-sec. The 1.5-sec. group and the "thousand" group were run by Margaret S. King. The data for the .5-sec. group were collected by C. A. Boneau in another study being carried on at the same time.

Quite obviously, the verbal reaction mediated the interstimulus interval quite effectively.

To one seeing this effect for the first time, the initial reaction is not apt to be one of surprise. For it is easy to see that saying the word "thousand" aloud is a means by which the subject can provide himself with another conditioned stimulus, at a more favorable interval for the occurrence of conditioning, specifically, the sound of the final *d* in the word thousand. So, one says, how does this differ from the reception of other stimulation, except perhaps in the uninteresting detail of being self-supplied? A moment's reflection, however, leads to the conclusion that this is exactly the point. The function of mediating reactions is simply that of providing one with cues in terms of which he may react in situations which would be difficult to deal with more directly.

The verbal mediation of generalized reactions

Potentially the most important demonstration of verbal mediation in classical conditioning is provided by the case of semantic
generalization in which the meaning of a stimulus provides the
basis for generalization. In some early studies of this phenomenon,
it was found that a response conditioned to a colored light, for
example, a blue light, generalized to the color name—in this case,
the word blue. In other cases, both the conditioned stimuli and the
generalized stimuli have been words. For our purposes here, the
most interesting work stems from that of Diven (1936), who reported that the Galvanic Skin Response conditioned to the word
"barn" generalized to other rural words. More recently, Lacey
and his associates (e.g., Lacey & Smith, 1954) have confirmed this
result. Subjects were required to free-associate for 15 sec. to each
word in a list containing, among others, the words "cow" and
"paper." For two different groups of subjects, a strong electric
shock followed one or the other of these words. The response employed was a change in heart rate. In addition to the words "cow"
and "paper," the list contained eight other words with rural connota-
tions; that is, words such as "plow," "corn," and "tractor."
Described briefly, the results of the investigation showed that the
subjects for whom "cow" and shock were paired developed a conditioned response to that word, and this response generalized to
the other rural words. Moreover, it was reported that both conditioning and generalization took place at a subconscious level.

More recently Chatterjee and Eriksen (1960) have repeated
the experiment employing the conditioned GSR as their response.
They also questioned the subjects somewhat more closely than
previous investigators had. Chatterjee and Eriksen found that,
under close questioning, the subjects were able to report degrees of
awareness which were sufficient to account for generalization of
the conditioned response. More specifically, the subjects frequently reported being uncertain whether a particular word was
followed by shock. These words tended to be viewed as dangerous
and to be responded to with a GSR, a conditioned response in the
case of the words "cow" or "paper" and a generalized response in
the case of the other words which he thought might be followed
by shock. Thus, the implications of this re-examination of the

Lacey and Smith result are (*a*) that the subjects were aware (correctly or incorrectly and to varying degrees) of the word-shock contingency, and (*b*) that this awareness was actually essential to the production of the results.

But it is important to note that the significance of these findings for our present discussion is not entirely clear. For one thing, the procedure in these experiments is extremely complicated and difficult to assign definitely either to the category of classical or instrumental conditioning. This is because there was an instrumental act (naming words) which was sometimes reinforced (by the omission of shock following nonshock words) after the manner of instrumental conditioning. On the other trials, however, shock followed the response without respect to the subject's behavior, something which is true of classical conditioning. As in the cases of verbal conditioning, it is probably important to make a sharp distinction between the reaction taken as an index of learning and the process itself. In the particular experiments under discussion here, it also seems important, again, to distinguish between the learning required to verbalize sequences of events and that which underlies the indicator response. It seems quite likely that the autonomic reactions measured in these experiments were the result of classical conditioning, and may have occurred in the absence of awareness in the same sense that other classical CR's may be established in this way. The generalization of these same reactions, however, were probably mediated by processes more or less accurately represented in awareness.

Summary and conclusions

The hypothesis of an effect upon behavior of events below the threshold of awareness has a long history in psychology, appearing importantly in the psychologies of Freud and James. For the purposes of this symposium, the ideas of James seem the more important. Present interest in the topic of learning without awareness seems directly traceable to James's ideas. More recently, however (judging from the various contributions to this symposium), there has developed a certain amount of controversy. As is always the case where such disputes exist, a part of what is argued seems to stem from definitional vagueness. For practical experimental purposes it has been necessary to equate awareness with the capability to verbalize certain events. This limits the breadth of the topic at the same time that it makes it empirically manageable.

Looking at the problem from the point of view of the traditional theorist of learning suggests several points which seem to be of value.

1. First, there is the trivial point that it seems unlikely that learning occurs at all in generally unaware subjects, such as those who are deeply asleep. If this is what is meant by learning without awareness, there is no secure evidence that such learning ever occurs. Experimenters in this area, however, define awareness somewhat differently, in terms of the recognition of certain experimentally arranged contingencies.

2. In the special case of classical conditioning, the evidence seems to indicate that the only item which probably has to be represented in awareness is the unconditioned stimulus, the reinforcer. Certain results of studies of perceptual learning indicate that even this awareness may not be necessary. The evidence on this point is sparse, however, and there is a question whether perceptual learning belongs to any of the recognized categories of learning. There is a suggestion here that our basic question (whether learning without awareness is possible) (a) may not be answerable until theorists of learning establish the limits of the process more definitely than is possible at present, and (b) that the answer may not be the same for all forms of learning.

3. Although classical conditioning is often thought of as a simple form of learning, it is actually a very complex process in which it is necessary to distinguish among (a) the hypothetical learning process (conditioning) which takes place, (b) the conditioned response which is the concrete actualization in performance of such learning, and (c) the ability, in the case of verbalizing subjects, to describe the sequence of stimuli in the experiment.

4. The interactions among these several subprocesses are even more complex, especially when these interactions are to be evaluated in terms of further considerations such as the extent to which they occur at a subconscious level. Such clarification as has been achieved in this paper suggests that most of what goes on in experiments on learning (even those which allegedly demonstrate learn-

ing without awareness) is represented in the subject's awareness. As mentioned in paragraph 2 above, the chief exceptions seem to occur in classical conditioning.

References

Chatterjee, B. B., & Eriksen, C. W.   Conditioning and generalization of GSR as a function of awareness. *J. abnorm. soc. Psychol.,* 1960, 60, 396-403.

Diven, K.   Certain determinants in the conditioning of anxiety reactions. *J. Psychol.,* 1936, 3, 291-308.

Grant, D. A., Riopelle, A. J., & Hake, H. W.   Resistance to extinction and the pattern of reinforcement: I. Alternation of reinforcement and the conditioned eyelid response. *J. exp. Psychol.,* 1950, 40, 53-60.

James, W.   *Principles of psychology.* New York: Holt, 1890.

Kimble, G. A.   *Hilgard and Marquis' Conditioning and learning.* (2nd. ed.) New York: Appleton-Century-Crofts, 1961.

Lacey, J. I., & Smith, R. L.   Conditioning and generalization of unconscious anxiety. *Science,* 1954, 120, 1045-1052.

Norris, E. B., & Grant, D. A.   Eyelid conditioning as affected by verbally induced inhibitory set and counter-reinforcement. *Amer. J. Psychol.,* 1948, 61, 37-49.

Razran, G.   A direct laboratory comparison of Pavlovian conditioning and traditional associative learning. *J. abnorm. soc. Psychol.,* 1955, 51, 649-652.

Razran, G.   The observable unconscious and the inferable conscious in current Soviet psychology: Interoceptive conditioning, semantic conditioning, and the orienting reflex. *Psychol. Rev.,* 1961, 68, 81-147.

Simon, C. W., & Emmons, W. H.   Responses to materials presented during various levels of sleep. *J. exp. Psychol.,* 1956, 51, 89-97.

What becomes of the input from the stimulus?[1]

Ernest R. Hilgard, *Stanford University*

Early behaviorists, troubled about introspection as an appropriate method for psychology, tried to get around the problem of awareness by dealing only with discrimination. Thus the "scientific" problem of perception rested for them upon the correlation between stimulus and response indicated in the act of discriminating, i.e., responding differently to the presence or absence of stimulation or in the presence of two unlike stimuli. Awareness, however, has another facet: the subject's awareness that he is discriminating. This is a puzzling problem in any case, no matter what one's relation to behaviorism. A sophisticated objectivism, in the form of operationism, is free to deal with this problem through converging operations (Garner, Hake, & Eriksen, 1956), but this freedom to work on the problem does not make its solution any easier.

The facts of perception force a few simple conclusions upon the investigator: (*a*) that much perception is highly correlated with the external stimulus, i.e., corresponds to reality, (*b*) that some perceptions which appear to be realistic are in fact distorted in one way or another, based on stimulus characteristics or on the subject's expectations, needs, wishes, or cognitive styles, and (*c*) that there are some perception-like cognitive experiences[2] that bear very little relation to external stimuli, and seem to reflect largely some kind of "state" of the person, as in dreams, hallucinations, and depersonalization. Experimental psychologists have dealt very largely with the first of these three sets of facts, somewhat with the

[1] The experiments on tachistoscopic perception referred to here were conducted in collaboration with Judah Landes, and supported by a grant from the Ford Foundation to R. R. Sears and E. R. Hilgard, which led to the establishment of the Laboratory of Human Development at Stanford.

[2] The word perception is usually confined to responses closely correlated with a presented stimulus, while cognition is a more general term which includes perception, judgment, imagery, and thought. The boundaries of what should be called perceptual are not clear in marginal cases.

second (particularly in the study of illusions), and very little with the third set, leaving these to abnormal psychology and the person-ologists. A division of labor is always acceptable and science need not be asked to deal with problems for which its methods are not yet suited. In the end, however, a complete science of psychology must eventually deal with the whole range of phenomena that are by common consent "psychological," and in the realm of awareness these include the peculiar cognitions included in the third class above.

An attempt to get at this unusual class of cognitive experiences descriptively was made several years ago by David Rapaport (1951, 1957). By carefully recording his hypnogogic states, dreams, and reveries, he detected and described a variety of states of consciousness that cannot well be classified as discriminations among stimuli. In reviewing some clinical cases of amnesia he pointed out a "dazed" state in which the person reacts somewhat automatically to the environment, guiding his movements by ex-ternal stimuli, but not aware of what he is doing, and not aware of the fact that he has lost his personal identity. This is followed by a "bewildered" state in which there is loss of personal identity, but the individual is aware of the loss and troubled by it, in turn fol-lowed by a return to "normal" (or relatively normal) in which personal identity is restored, even though there may still be some gaps in memory, particularly for the events of the first stage. A full psychology of awareness must take into account the aware-nesses implied in these descriptions.

The present paper does not deal with this full range of prob-lems, but is concerned instead with the effects of stimulation at or near threshold, where the problems of awareness (other than self-awareness) most often intrude themselves into the interpretation of psychological data. The stimulus is the entering wedge into per-ception, and we shall be concerned with how stimulus input is processed in the act of perceiving; the aspects of this process that are least stimulus-bound throw some light on the larger problems of awareness.

When a stimulus is not identified

Let us suppose that a subject is confronted with a visual stimu-lus pattern that under normal circumstances he could identify. For example, if in a book or magazine under ordinary illumination he saw a line drawing of a building or a boat or a mountain, he could tell you what he saw. This involves memory, categorizing, and verbal labeling, but these are commonplace tasks if he "perceives" the picture. These extra tasks, what Bruner (1957a) calls "going beyond the information given," are essential parts of the cognitive process, and they are often overlooked when perception is realistic because there is such a high correlation between stimulus and response. Under what circumstances will a stimulus pattern such as those described *not* be identified? This implies one kind of definition of subliminal: a presentation of an identifiable stimulus under circumstances such that it is not identified.

1. *Below registration level.* The concept of an absolute threshold can be pushed to the point that there is no physiological consequence whatever of the presented stimulus. This we shall call the "threshold of registration." This is a very low threshold, with stimulus energy close to that required to set off a discharge in a single rod or cone. Psychophysical experiments seldom measure this threshold, though they get very close to it (Blackwell, 1952, 1953). When this very low threshold is meant, something subliminal does not have any effect upon the organism, and there is no input from the stimulus except to the superficial portions of the receptor system.

2. *Above registration level, but below detection level.* The problem of threshold measurement has led to a relativistic conception of the threshold that goes by the name of the detection level, which, for sake of parallelism, we may call the "threshold of detection." This implies that all stimuli have to be picked out against a background that is "noisy" in the communication sense of the term; that is, there are intrinsic effects in the eye (Eigenlicht) that provide a confusing background against which threshold lights have to be perceived, and our own breathing and circulation of blood can be heard in a soundproof room when we are listening for threshold sounds. In more practical settings, such as listening to conversations at a cocktail party, or seeing the blips on a radar screen, the "signal" is often in severe competition with other events. Those who favor the detection analysis are inclined to deny that there is such a thing as a sensory threshold (Swets, 1961).

Now the subject may be unable to identify the stimulus that is presented, but it has perhaps registered in some manner, so that we are no longer free to judge that because it is subliminal (by detection criteria) it is without effect. There has been input from the stimulus.[3]

3. *Above detection level, but below identification level.* There is the in-between case in which the subject clearly perceives "a something" but is unable to identify it. The usual circumstances are that the pattern is too small, too far away, too faint, or too briefly exposed. Here also there has been input from the stimulus, an input that commonly yields usable information (Bricker & Chapanis, 1953).

4. *Above identification level, but masked by contiguous stimulation.* I wish to distinguish between this case and the preceding ones by citing two forms of stimulation that cause normally identifiable stimulus patterns to fall below the level of awareness (possibly below detection as well as identification). One is simultaneous presentation of a visual pattern to both eyes in a stereoscope. In that case there is no doubt but that registration takes place, one stimulus registering by way of one retina, the other registering by way of the other; yet we know from old experiments on binocular rivalry and from more recent experiments with meaningful stimuli that one stimulus pattern may block out awareness of the other (e.g., Engel, 1956; Bagby, 1957; Pettigrew, Allport, & Barnett, 1958; Davis, 1959; Hastorf & Myro, 1959). The second form is that of successive stimulation. When one stimulus is presented briefly (but at an exposure that would be long enough for it to be identified) and is followed immediately by the presentation of another stimulus, at longer exposure, only the second is reported. The method was developed by Werner (1935) and Cheatham (1952), and used more recently by Smith and Henriksson (1955), Klein, Spence, Holt, and Gourevitch (1958), and Eagle (1959).

Under these circumstances we have little doubt about the full registration of the stimulus, yet it is unreported by the subject and is in that sense subliminal.

[3] The question whether or not input is blocked off by some sort of gating mechanism before reaching the cortex can be raised; I am avoiding the issues in a contemporary physiology of perception (e.g., Bruner, 1957b).

5. *Below identification level because of adverse characteristics of the subject.* The fifth class of nonperceived stimuli includes those that would be above the level of identification except that the subject is preoccupied, tired, drugged, or perhaps "defended" against the stimulus. I do not propose to review the literature on perceptual defense but the issue is not yet closed, and it remains highly plausible that there are circumstances under which the subject's personal history will modify the thresholds for identification of a stimulus (Eriksen, 1960; Lowenfeld, 1961).

Just as the word "registration" has been used to indicate an input above the registration threshold, whether or not it is perceived, the word "activation" (following Klein, 1959) can be used for a detectable influence of the stimulus by the subject. In all of the above cases, other than the first, there has been registration, and where there has been registration, there may be activation. The issue of subliminal stimulation is thus taken out of anything mysterious or anything a priori improbable, and it becomes an empirical problem to indicate the evidences for activation when the stimulus is unrecognized and hence out of clear awareness.

It should be noted that there are marginal cases that do not fall easily into any one of the classes. One such case is the stimulus that is incidental, so that one is only dimly aware of it, as in the case of a striking clock, whose strokes we can occasionally count, even though we were not at first paying attention to them. If we cannot recover them, they were in some sense subliminal; if we can, they were supraliminal. Another case has to do with incomplete perception, when a total stimulus is perceived but parts of it ignored. For the present, however, we may accept these classes as five cases in which we do not know what we saw, even though in four of the cases the stimulus registered and perhaps activated us in some way.

How activation from unidentified stimulus patterns may be manifested

After registration comes activation. Activation can bring above threshold some derivative of the stimulus input in a number of ways; to the extent that these derivatives can be established we have learned something about what happens to a registered stimulus that has not been perceived. Here there are at least five kinds of indicators that have been used.[4]

1. *Guessing.* A threshold of recognition or identification is indeed a threshold, and events that are near the threshold can be brought above it in various ways. When there is some information in the stimulus, but not enough for identification, identification can often be achieved by reducing the alternatives and having the subject select from among them. His "guessing" is facilitated by the information he has received (Adams, 1957; Bricker & Chapanis, 1953; Goldberg & Fiss, 1959; Spence, 1961). Note that this interpretation is that subliminal activation acts the same as supraliminal stimulation, and the resultant perception is a decision based on probabilities. It is the same sort of explanation as that used for the ability to recognize a word in a tachistoscope at an exposure time such that individual letters cannot be read.

2. *Word associations.* Free word associations represent a kind of noncommittal process in which anything goes. The consequence might be something like guessing, without the subject taking responsibility for his guesses, so that some kind of context created by what was registered influences what is yielded in word association. In some recent experiments modeled upon experiments of Shevrin and Luborsky and Shevrin and Stross,[5] but using words where they used pictures, Spence (1961) found that the subliminal words BEE and GUN, in one instance, and SUCK and SEED, in another, led to the nonchance selection of related words from a list of words supposedly included in a somewhat vague exposure that had masked the subliminal words. This is somewhat like guessing, point 1 above, but the guesses included some derivatives that did not directly reflect the presented stimuli. Verbal responses in experiments such as those of Pine (1960) and Bach (1959) show the influences of incidentally perceived words, although the connections are sometimes a little remote.

[4] A very thorough review of perceptual indicators by Goldiamond (1958) relates them in a meaningful way to contemporary psychophysics. He points out many of the common sources of error in experiments on subliminal perception.

[5] Shevrin, H., & Luborsky, L. Displacement mechanisms in a state of reduced awareness. Unpublished manuscript, 1958. Shevrin, H., & Stross, L. The fate of fleeting impressions in dreams, waking images, and hypnosis. Unpublished manuscript, 1961.

3. *Fantasy productions.* Fantasy productions are of various kinds, such as stories to TAT cards (Pine, 1960), or drawings of primed or unprimed images. Primed images are those that are suggested when the subject has done something else, such as responding in a word-association test, or been given some kind of hint, perhaps through a word list; unprimed images result when he is free to fantasy anything and to try to draw what appears. The drawings of fantasied pictures under these two circumstances have been widely used to detect activation by unnoticed features of a stimulus, e.g., Allers and Teler (1924), Fisher (1956), Hilgard (1958), Fisher and Paul (1959), and Paul and Fisher (1959). Most investigators report positive results, but the results have to be interpreted with some caution. A useful review, sensitive to the issues involved, is that of Fisher (1960b).

4. *Dreams.* Dreams are special kinds of fantasy productions. The early experiments of Poetzl (1917) showed recovery of un- noticed features of visually presented stimuli in dreams, and his lead has been followed by others, notably Malamud and Linder (1931), Fisher (1954, 1956, 1960a), and Shevrin and Luborsky (1958). The results are, in general, similar to those found in waking fantasy. Careful examination by Johnson & Eriksen (1961) of the results of Shevrin and Luborsky casts some doubt upon the statistical significance of their findings; because theirs is the only series in repetition of Poetzl that has thus far attempted statistical control, it leaves the whole matter a little uncertain from a quantitative scientific standpoint.

5. *Influence upon some secondary cognitive task.* If a reg- istered but unnoticed stimulus results in activation, this result may be shown indirectly by influence on some other cognitive activity. Thus in several experiments the subliminal presentation of affec- tively toned words led to a corresponding affective interpretation of neutral stimuli (Smith, Spence, & Klein, 1959; Eagle, 1959; Goldstein & Barthol, 1960). In another study, subliminally pre- sented representations of male and female genitalia led to mascu- line or feminine identifications of otherwise ambiguous human faces (Klein *et al.,* 1958). It was not necessary for there to be any recollection, recognition, or recovery of the stimulus originally out

of awareness for this influence to be inferred from the other responses of the subject.

We now have before us some essential conditions, first, under which a registered stimulus may remain unperceived, and second, under which activation by such an unperceived stimulus may be revealed. This leaves us with the empirical problems of criticism and replication of reported results, and the theoretical problems of interpreting the results that we accept as substantiated.

Some aftereffects of vaguely perceived pictures

Before turning to some theoretical problems of how stimulus input becomes incorporated into realistic perceptions or fantasy productions, I wish to discuss briefly some of the findings from an experiment in our laboratory.[6] If I stress some of our difficulties, it is only to warn that the critics of experiments of this kind are not being excessively pedantic; to convert what is plausible to what is proven is very difficult in investigations of marginal perceptual phenomena.

We designed an experiment of the Allers and Teler (1924) type in which, after a brief exposure of visual stimuli (colored slides of two scenes, one an Indian family in the southwest, another a jungle scene), subjects were asked to draw pictures aroused by a succession of association words. A number of controls were built in to improve upon the original experiments and upon the repetition by Luborsky and Shevrin (1956) and Shevrin and Luborsky (1958).

Among the features included in the design were: (*a*) the use of two pictures followed by the same set of stimulus words to elicit word associations, in order to detect to what extent the fantasies were functions of the words, to what extent functions of the pictures (the single subject did not of course have the same set of words for both pictures, but two sets of words were counterbalanced); (*b*) the use of both pictures in direct and in mirror-image presentations (obverse and reverse, in the terminology of medals and coins) so that recall of perceived parts could be identified by orientation as well as by substance; (*c*) in every case original and final drawings

---

[6] Some of the findings have been presented in preliminary form in Hilgard (1958), but the full report of the experiments has not been published pending opportunity to gather some additional data and to complete some additional controls.

of what the subject perceived the stimulus picture to be; (*d*) recognition tests in which the perceived picture had to be selected from variants in which details were altered; (*e*) enough subjects (a total of 64) so that something could be asserted about the frequency of whatever effects were found.

There was no effort to make the pictures subliminal, in the sense that nothing could be detected or recognized; the illumination and exposure-time (.01 sec.) permitted the subject to see something, occasionally a great deal, but plenty of details were missing to give room for "recovery" of unnoticed material.

We were looking for "recovery" of unnoticed material in one form or another, either in direct recovery (placing in a later drawing something missing from the original drawing), or in indirect recovery through some kind of transformation (as in a puzzle picture, in which a shadow might become a dog, or in some sort of influence upon a later picture that could be attributed to some unnoticed feature of an earlier one).

As soon as we began scoring the pictures we found that the scoring task was much more difficult than anticipated. Direct recoveries were very few indeed; that is, there seldom appeared in a later picture some feature unnoticed in the original unmistakably in its right place and in its right size. Some features scorable as direct recoveries were very suspect, because some elaborations or decorations can easily appear, as when a house without windows has windows placed in it in a later drawing, in purely conventional positions, or when a man seated out of doors without a hat has a hat added in a later picture. Such elaborations are scorable because the original house *did* have windows and the man *did* have a hat; they are scored as recoveries provided the judge detects features that convince him there is some specific relation to the original stimulus. This kind of thing plagues these studies; only a probability estimate will serve to protect against assuming a connection where there is none. A commonly proposed control, of free fantasy without a stimulus picture, does not do; a house will not be there in the original fantasied picture as often as it was found in our sample (where a house had been noted), so that the recovery of windows will not be as frequent either. A statistically significant difference between experimental and control results can be found without the difference being meaningful.[7]

The word-association method of fantasy arousal produces additional difficulties of estimating probabilities. We had thought that the use of the same list of words with both pictures would correct for the influence of the word itself, but we found the response words to be very often different following the Indian picture and the jungle picture; thus the word "water" was more frequently followed by the word "waterfall" in the context of the jungle picture, and the drawing of a waterfall was unique to the jungle picture. An unperceived waterfall in the picture could have been influential, and hence the drawing of a waterfall was scorable as a stimulus recovery. The "control" by way of the Indian picture was adequate: "waterfall" and the drawing of a waterfall did not occur in recovery following the stimulus-word "water." In fact, however, the Indian scene was one that looked hot and dry, even when poorly perceived, and the word "water" was more likely to lead to "dry" or "drought" than to "waterfall." Hence the control was not really a satisfactory one.

The better control was the mirror-image of the same picture; now if the waterfalls following the jungle picture in two forms are oriented correctly, then they are more likely to be recoveries. Here one has to be careful to subtract the improperly oriented ones from the correct ones; counting only the positive indicators is one of the errors that besets experiments on subliminal perception (Goldiamond, 1958). These controls turned out quite well, although there is so much idiosyncrasy in response that it takes a very large number of subjects before there are many genuine mirror-image drawings to compare. There were a total of nine waterfall recoveries scored as probable among the 64 subjects, six of these following the stimulus-word "water," three following other words ("white," "happy," and "afraid"). Six followed the obverse stimuli, three the reverse. Only two were associated with the response word "waterfall." Of these nine, seven were oriented properly, one (from obverse exposure) was directly opposite to what it

---

[7] The blank stimulus is more appropriate as a control when the comparison is with a stimulus intended to be entirely subliminal, but if one supposes that there is always *some* information from a stimulus sufficiently intense to register, similar considerations apply. In that case any later fantasies should be compared with immediate ones, and scoring difficulties such as we faced may also occur.

should have been, and the other (from a reverse exposure) was ambiguous, but it was properly oriented when incorporated in the final drawing. Thus the score of seven out of nine correct and one ambiguous gives support to the judgment that the waterfalls were in fact influenced by the unnoticed features of the stimulus pictures.

The control through the use of mirror-image pictures did not work very well, in general, for two reasons. The first reason, already mentioned, is that there was such variety in response that classification of responses into frequency categories, while feasible, resulted usually in very few responses in each category. The second reason is that most recoveries, with the conspicuous exception of the waterfalls, were fitted into a scene that was already oriented, so that the statistical finding of correct orientation would be meaningless. For example, if a man seated on the left (in one orientation) gets a hat, and the same man seated on the right (in the reverse orientation) also gets a hat, this meets the criteria of correct orientation, but as long as there is only one man the value as evidence of recovery is no better than if the two recoveries had been similarly oriented. Saying that the control did not work well means only that it did not help very much in substantiating the fact of recovery; the control did not, however, provide any evidence to detract from the impression that the recoveries were genuine.

The controls through mirror-image exposures would have worked better had there been more conspicuous recoveries, so that probabilities could have been better established. (Had we had twenty waterfalls instead of nine we could have computed more meaningful statistics about their orientation.) Careful examination of reports in experiments of this kind show that dramatic recoveries are very few indeed; hence, either extremely large samples will be needed or other methods used. There is, however, a good deal that can be learned about the nature of perception and fantasy formation from what happened, apart from the demonstration of direct stimulus recovery. It is these other things that I wish to emphasize in summarizing some of our findings. My cautions have to do primarily with the frequencies of effects, most of which have enough uncertainty that one can easily reduce the counted recoveries or magnify their number; in a few cases the qualitative results are so striking that one feels confident that *some* recovery is not illusory.

Let me review some of our findings:

1. *Scoring reliability.* The scoring for recovery, which requires a comparison of later drawings with that made just after the stimulus exposure, proved very difficult, apart from the problem of whether a scorable recovery was genuinely a recovery and not a lucky invention or importation. After failure to agree in some preliminary scoring, then preparing a careful code and working together on half the sample, the second half of the sample, scored entirely independently by two judges, yielded reliability coefficients expressed as tetrachoric correlations of $r_t = .72$ for the drawings following exposure of the Indian picture and $r_t = .76$ for the jungle picture. These are based on the presence or absence of one or more scorable "recoveries" in any of the six pictures that were drawn following word associations after the exposure of the picture; the unit is the subject, not the picture.

2. *Frequency of probable recoveries.* After comparing notes and agreeing upon scores, we judged 28 per cent of the subjects to have shown one or more scorable (probable) recoveries on the Indian picture and 36 per cent one or more recoveries on the jungle picture. We have no way of knowing just how much these should be discounted, but they represent features of the original stimulus absent in the original drawing that appeared (whether by recovery or by luck) in some later picture; the judges thought the pictured additions were specific enough to be indicative of influence by the original stimulus. If one counts various kinds of more remote symbolic representation, these scores would be much higher, at least doubled in frequency.[8]

3. *Subject consistency with two stimulus pictures.* There was some individual consistency in recovery, yielding a correlation of $r = .23$ between weighted recovery scores for Indian and jungle, respectively. With a sample of 64 this does not reach a satisfactory significance level, however; even if a relationship is accepted it may indicate only that certain free drawing styles, common to both pictures, occasionally led to the report of recovery on both pictures, whereas constricted styles did not.

[8] This estimate is based on including in our scores a "doubtful" recovery category that was less stringent than the "probable" category.

4. *Idiosyncratic word associations and recovery.* Another stylistic feature that was related to scorable recoveries was the kind of response given to the word-association test. If we consider as a common response the responses given by 10 per cent or more of the Minnesota standardization sample to the Kent-Rosanoff words that were included in our stimulus lists (Russell & Jenkins, 1954) then we find that those who gave fewer common responses tended more often to give scorable recoveries, a result that we had predicted (chi-square, 3.9; $p = .05$, two-tailed). Again, however, the relationship is a marginal one, and subject to more than one interpretation. Thus the idiosyncratic response may have shown that the stimulus word tapped something in the motivational-affective system of the person, and thus encouraged fantasy, or it may have been that the subject, thinking about the picture, was led to give a response more specific to the picture, and hence more likely to lead to importation into the picture of something scorable. (A response specific to a picture has a higher probability of being idiosyncratic than a response to the stimulus word alone.)

5. *Relevant stimulus words as priming recovery.* Some of the stimulus words were more relevant to the Indian picture, some to the jungle picture. Three graduate students rated the stimulus words for relevance to the pictures, and their agreements were so high that an ordering could be made. Thus stimulus words such as "house" and "boy" were judged highly relevant to the Indian family seated in front of a building, while "afraid" and "water" had little relevance to this happy and dry scene. Correspondingly, "tree" and "water" were highly relevant for the jungle scene, while "white" and "child" had little to do with it. The recoveries recorded were significantly related to the relevance of the stimulus words, the high-relevance words yielding recoveries more often than the medium and low words. The differences between high and low words were satisfactorily significant (C. R. for Indians, 3.18; for jungle, 2.77). Again we do not know just what effect this priming may have had in adding relevant material to the drawn picture that then was scored as recovery. It may be noted that in their original study, Allers and Teler often used highly relevant stimulus words.

6. *Thematic relevance of response drawing in relation to recovery.* When the subject drew a picture following the word association, the picture was sometimes relevant to the picture seen, sometimes not. Again, the more relevant the picture, the more likely a scorable recovery; the result proved significant with the jungle picture ($p = .03$), not with Indians. Here is a troublesome problem for the scorer: if the theme of the picture is changed, how accurate does some feature have to be for it to be recognized as a recovery? When the original man in the Indian picture puts on a hat, this is scored as recovery. Suppose there is substituted for him a man out fishing in a rowboat, and he puts on a hat in a later picture. Is that scorable? Note that in raising these questions I am not implying an answer; the question is not so much one of what may be happening as one of how to score so as to be sure that what is happening is what is inferred. There is no way of knowing (without appropriate controls) whether or not, in fact, the hat on the fisherman is related to the hat that may have registered but gone unnoticed in the flashed picture.

7. *Equivalence of responses to obverse and reverse pictures.* The obverse and reverse pictures yield similar recovery patterns following the word associations. For the Indian picture, for example, the relative order of effectiveness of the stimulus words in yielding scorable recoveries is represented by a rho of $+.86$. Similarly the relative frequency of categories (baby, hat, window, etc.) in which recovery is found correlates rho $= +.73$. The corresponding correlations following the jungle picture were $+.44$ and $+.71$. (The use of obverse-reverse as a control was illustrated above.)

There is order in the findings, but much of this lawfulness is contributed by features of the recovery situation rather than by features of the exposed stimulus in which we were primarily interested; the influence of various factors on what a subject draws is clear enough, but it is difficult to assign the fraction that belongs to recovery of unperceived features of the stimulus.

So much for some of the quantitative findings. They are often interesting, but are very uncertain with respect to the basic problem of how the unperceived aspects of the exposed picture influenced the later productions.

8. *Qualitative findings: A typical "good" recovery sequence.*
It is possible to select sequences that are convincing in showing
that some genuine "recovery" takes place. Consider the sequence
shown in Figure 1. Here the original drawing of the Indians is
that of three somewhat vague adult figures and a baby, in front of
a building (or wall) with horizontal lines, but without windows.
To the stimulus-word "boy" the subject replies "man" and draws
a man figure resembling in many respects the man in the picture;
later, when asked to draw what he saw originally, the man as
drawn is a little sketchy, but he wears his hat and there is a
window, not properly placed, but with its location perhaps suggested by the log-end appearing in the original above the baby.
This is the kind of series scored rather confidently as recovery.

Exposed Picture

Original Drawing

Boy-"Man"

Final Drawing

Figure 1. Illustration of recovery and inclusion of recovered material in
final drawing.

The original Indian picture (actually a colored photographic slide) is indicated, followed by tracings of the drawings of a single subject. The original
drawing followed the brief exposure of the picture; the drawing of the man
was made after the association "man" was given to the stimulus "boy." The
final drawing was an attempt at the end to draw the originally exposed picture; note that the man wears a hat and a window appears.

The criticism might be made that the original drawing was incomplete, a kind of diagram of what the subject saw, without recorded details. According to this view, he simply added features artistically in the later drawing: it is artistically more complete, but may not represent any genuine recovery. One reply is that the subject appeared to try to tell everything he could about the original, and nothing that he said showed that he had details that he failed to draw; we know, however, that it is hard to put fleeting impressions into words.

9. *A recognition test as a control on failure to report.* We included a recognition test in our experiment in order to check in part this question of lack of skill in reporting (or drawing) what was perceived.[9] A striking result of this recognition test was that when presented with distorted versions of the picture (modeled after what pretest subjects had drawn), subjects more often chose a version that had not been presented than the true version that they had seen. A total of 28 out of 32 (88 per cent) chose an altered Indian picture in preference to the exposed one, and 23 of 32 (72 per cent) chose an altered jungle picture in preference to the one most like that which they had seen. In the Indian picture the correct version took fifth place in the recognition test out of six pictures presented. While, in the jungle picture, the correct version was chosen more often than the distorted versions, it was chosen by but 9 of the 32 subjects, and the next two versions were chosen by 7 each. These results convinced us that the perception itself was commonly inaccurate, and that we were not dealing with problems created by inability to describe or to draw. The reason for the poorer showing of the Indian picture on the recognition test was easy to discern: subjects preferred a picture better structured than the original. They preferred a picture in which the half-hidden girl in the middle of the picture was either brought into full view, or left out of the picture.

10. *Failure to include recovery in the final drawing.* What appeared to be a good recovery within the word-association series often was not included in the final drawing, when the attempt was made to reproduce the originally exposed picture. The series in Figure 1 shows recovery plus inclusion; that in Figure 2 shows

[9] Because the recognition test was used with only half the subjects, $N = 32$.

Exposed Picture

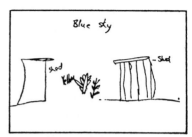

Original Drawing

Water-"Waterfall"

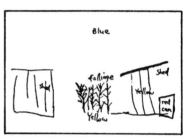

Final Drawing

Figure 2. Illustration of recovery without inclusion of the recovered material in the final drawing.

The original jungle picture (again a colored photographic slide) is sketched for comparison with the drawings of one subject. The original drawing distorts the theme, but preserves some of the masses of the original picture. The next drawing, following the response "waterfall" to the word "water," is a faithful representation of the unperceived waterfall in the original. In the final drawing of the originally exposed picture the waterfall does not appear.

recovery without inclusion. After a very skimped original drawing, which reflects none of the jungle character, the stimulus-word "water" yields the response "waterfall" in the original drawing. But when the final drawing is made, the return is essentially to the original drawing.[10]

The fact that recovery made in the word-association drawings may or may not be included in the final drawing, and that occasionally recoveries show in the final drawing that do not appear in the word-association drawings, raises the question of a merely

[10] When I showed this drawing to Dr. Charles Fisher he noted that the misspelled word "folliage" in the final drawing might be interpreted as a condensation from "fall" in "waterfall," and the greater density of the shrubbery in the final drawing some further indication of an influence from the intervening drawing. Such possibilities cannot be denied, but their value as evidence is slight.

reminiscent type of recovery as against a primed recovery via word-associations. A plausible assumption is as follows: if the recovery is of the reminiscent type, it ought to be retained, and appear in the final drawing; it may appear in the final drawing even though it did not appear in the word-association series. If it is of the primed type, it might appear following word associations but go unrecognized, and hence not be placed in the final drawing. If we use this criterion to distinguish between reminiscence and the purer instances of primed recoveries,[11] we find that there were 5 subjects among 64 (8 per cent) who had scorable probable recoveries within word associations, following exposure of the Indian picture, who did *not* have any evidence of scorable recovery in the final drawing. These are then cases of pure primed recovery, without the reminiscent character. There were 15 cases (23 per cent) following the jungle picture who had primed recoveries that were not included in the final drawings. On the whole, about half of the scorable recovery responses were of this kind. These recoveries were not recognized as having belonged to the originally exposed picture; it may be argued either that they were not true recoveries, or that they were in some sense dissociated from the original stimulus. It seems highly plausible that there were at least some derivatives from the originally exposed picture that went unrecognized by the subject. The subjects themselves often commented with surprise on the similarities between some of their products and the original pictures (after the experiment was over and they saw the original), but this means only that they had not previously seen the connection; it gives no assurance that the connection was not fortuitous.

11. *Distortions of previously perceived features of the stimulus.* Another observation should be made about things that happened within the experiment that had nothing to do with the original hypotheses being tested. This is the tendency for parts of the picture that *were* noticed to reappear in thinly disguised form in some of the later fantasies. This is not scorable as the recovery of unnoticed features of the stimulus, but it is interesting in terms of the mechanisms of fantasy production. Thus the baby in white,

[11] This somewhat underplays the primed recovery, because priming could facilitate reminiscence and the primed picture could thus be carried along into later drawings.

against a background of a mother's very black dress, occasionally gave rise to fantasies of snow-covered mountains, with the snowy peak on a volcanic mountain drawn in the part of the picture where the baby's white had been. The swaddled baby (although seen as such) became in another instance a grown man in a barber's chair, with the barber's cloth tucked carefully around him. Thus fantasy production showed an influence from what had been perceived, but the original drawing was more veridical than the one based on fantasy influenced by the exposed stimulus.

In summary, a good deal can be found out in experiments of this kind about perceptual distortions and fantasy, even though there are lingering uncertainties about the nature of recovery of unnoticed material.

Does activation by registered but unperceived stimuli follow the same rules as ordinary perception?

This question has recently been raised by Donald Spence (1961) who suggests that some experiments indicate that subliminal perception is continuous with supraliminal. Thus a subliminal adjective may influence the interpretation of a supraliminal picture just as it might if that word were attached to the picture and both were given ample exposure; an ambiguous stimulus is reinterpreted in accordance with subliminal stimuli as it might be through providing a specific "set" or other context. Thus subliminal activation may be part of the probabilistic background, just as memory, expectation, prior response, and other supplements to the presented stimulus are. If other probabilistic features are strong enough, the subliminal stimulus itself may be identified; if it is part of the background for a second stimulus its influence may be detected by what it does to the identification of the second stimulus.

The second possibility is that the rules for subliminal activation are different. This is implied in the psychoanalytic distinction between primary and secondary process, a distinction that has served to guide many of the recent experiments on subliminal activation. The distinction, while somewhat unclear, is an attempt to deal with genuine problems, and should probably be taken more seriously by the general psychologist (Hilgard, 1962). Those who are convinced that primary-process thinking follows rules different from those of secondary process believe that they have evidence that incidental stimuli appear in more transformed forms than central ones (Pine, 1960), and that they enter into cognition by way of drive-organized memories rather than by way of conceptually organized ones (Fisher, 1960a). Spence (1961) believed his results to show that the rules of both primary and secondary process apply in subthreshold stimulation, the effect being determined by additional variables.

The Freudian distinction between primary and secondary process has many facets that are bound with other features of the metapsychology, but the distinction is useful apart from its embeddedness in the more general theory. Related features have been noted in one form or another by other writers on cognition. Thus the Leipzig school of *Aktualgenese* ("microgenesis") has for many years made much of vague and amorphous perceptions that only gradually become elaborated and structured to correspond with external reality. The "endogenous" determinants are gradually replaced by "exogenous" determinants; endogenous being more like drive-organization (primary process) and exogenous like conceptual or reality organization (secondary process). The work of Krueger, Undeutsch, Sander, and others goes back many years (Flavell & Draguns, 1957).

Let us try to conceptualize what happens in coping with an ambiguous stimulus presentation, such as our briefly exposed picture, and how such a presentation contributes to fantasy production.

1. An ordinary supraliminal stimulus that serves as information about external reality is fitted into cognitive structure and identified by the ordinary processes of recognized similarity with prior experience, categorizing, and responding appropriately, thus providing confirmation of the perceptual result through reality testing. If the stimulus is somewhat ambiguous, there may be decision processes involved, which are like probabilistic gambling, but the end process is a definite percept. This is the functionalist interpretation of perception, which is similar to the Freudian secondary process.

2. In this process of conceptualizing and categorizing, some information from the stimulus is lost, even though this additional information may have registered. Thus the structure into which

the stimulus pattern is fitted may not have a place for some of the incongruities of the stimulus, which are then lost to awareness.

Briefly exposed pictures are often thematically perceived, but the theme may be a wrong one. Our Indians sometimes became Iowa farmers, and then pitchforks and other American farm paraphernalia appeared. The jungle scene became a southern California garden scene, with no place for a waterfall (though there sometimes was a fountain added). When a wrong theme is the basis for the cognitive structure, more of the original elements are usually incongruous than when an appropriate theme is chosen, although the picture itself may contain incongruous elements. For example, three soft-drink bottles in the Indian picture, two held by children and one standing on the ground, were never perceived.[12] This is not because they were too faint to be seen, but because they were not perceptually congruous with an Indian picture. When 4 x 6 inch reproductions of the picture are passed around a room, with ample time to view the pictures, the bottles also go unnoticed, though they are easily seen when attention is called to them. We are left with the problem of what becomes of these fragments; the Freudian theory has a primary process to make use of them.

3. It may be conjectured that incidental or unnoticed stimulation (registration below the level of identification for whatever reason) acts just the same as the unnoticed features of supraliminal stimulation. This interpretation leaves us with a common problem of interpretation of some features of subliminal and supraliminal activation.

4. Some unassimilated material may simply be dissipated and lost. One possibility is that it has some sort of output through muscular tension and affective response, without any clear cognitive output. It seems most unlikely that every bit of incidental stimulation is recorded and stored as a cognitive product; some of it probably evaporates in another form.

5. Some unassimilated material remains in readiness for assimilation to cognitive structure. If it is registered below detection and identification levels it may still be active, along with incongruous material that has been excluded from the pattern to which it belonged in stimulation because that pattern became too

[12] Unfortunately, an excellent opportunity for "recovery" was also missed, for there was very little evidence of any activation by these unnoticed bottles.

highly structured. Note that we have to be concerned both with the assimilation of unassimilated material to structures, and with the spinning off of some material when assimilation occurs. The essence of the "mobile cathexis" of Freudian primary process is that something is lying around that has to get discharged, so that it may attach itself to an idea to which it did not originally belong. The readiness for assimilation to structures would account for the influence of unassimilated registered material upon other ambiguous stimulus material in the process of becoming structured. The assimilated material may be transformed so as to be coherent with a structure in process of consolidating, or a structure that is formed may be altered to be coherent with the stimulus material. The mechanics of this process cannot be specified, but there is some tendency toward coherent structures that can be recognized. One emphasis upon microgenesis in perception is upon the fact that the act of cognition takes time, as pointed out by Smith (1957). The categorizing of a stimulus is affected not only by prior set but by a set that is introduced after the stimulus has been presented (Lawrence & Coles, 1954). Thus a full act of cognition may rework sensory data that have not yet entered into a firm cognitive structure.

It is the Freudians who have pointed out a persistence of some of the unassimilated results of stimulation over longer time, such as a day or a week. These unassimilated materials are found appearing as day-residues in dreams or in fantasy.

We are led to conjecture at least a two-fold process in perception: the prompt assimilation of data from stimulation to cognitive structures (schemata, Gestalten, or cell assemblies), and some pool of fragments from prior registration of stimuli that remain unassimilated, these fragments persisting in time, but with a readiness for structure-formation. Thus we arrive at a distinction not too unlike the Freudian one between primary and secondary process. The distinction between primary and secondary process is as good a conceptualization as we possess of this problem.

Freud proposed that one manifestation of primary-process thinking was hallucinations, the dream furnishing the chief evidence. If we think of all imaginative productions as belonging to the same family, we might propose that the kind of structure that furnishes the best outlet for the variety of fragments unassimilated into cognitive structures is indeed the fantasy production. Just as a kaleidoscope can incorporate odd pieces of broken glass into pleasant patterns, so the fantasy structure can pick up fragments and relate them meaningfully. Here is where other features of Freudian theory have something to say (e.g., wish fulfilment). It is not surprising that ambiguous TAT cards are more influenced by unnoticed accompanying words than less ambiguous cards (Goldstein & Barthol, 1960). The presumption is that fitting together of unassimilated fragments is easier the more fluid the cognitive structure in process of formation.[13]

This formulation leaves much to be desired in the way of precision. I suppose the main point is that in both veridical perception and fantasy-making the results of stimulation are manipulated in ways that are not represented in awareness; this, rather than the problem of sensory thresholds, is the one to which we need to address ourselves if we are eventually to understand awareness.

Summary

A fully adequate theory of awareness must include not only the act of discriminating events, but the subject's awareness that he is discriminating. The effects of stimulation near the threshold are attempts to get at a part of this problem, though not all of it. A stimulus may be unperceived because it is below registration level, between registration and detection levels, between detection and identification levels, masked by contiguous stimulation, or below identification level because of adverse characteristics of the percipient. In all cases except the first there is registration of the stimulus, and there is no a priori reason why this registration should not have detectable effects.

Activation by registered but unperceived stimuli is reflected in a number of ways, by guessing, through word associations, in

[13] My guess is that a functionalistic or probabilistic explanation could be made to cover fantasy formation along the same lines as an explanation of ordinary veridical perception. In both cases the structure that is favored depends upon a resolution or compromise based on the ambiguity of the stimulus, the drives, preoccupations, and the residues from prior stimulation and response. Projective test interpretations are based on such considerations. Thus a uniform theory of cognitive structure formation might be developed, covering both ordinary perception and the construction of fantasies.

fantasy productions, in dreams, and in influences upon some secondary cognitive task.

Experiments are reported in which, with 64 subjects, the brief exposure of colored pictures was followed by an original drawing, a series of drawings of fantasies primed by word associations, and a final drawing. The effort was to detect "recoveries" of unnoticed material from the originally exposed stimulus picture. While an appreciable number of such recoveries were noted, the problems of scoring and control make the assigning of precise quantitative values very difficult. There were a number of orderly relationships between scorable recoveries and the features of the words used to elicit word associations followed by the drawings in which the recoveries were found.

The results of these experiments, and the many related experiments reported in recent years, suggest an interpretation of the processes of perception along the following lines: (a) The usual act of perception rapidly assimilates perceptual input to cognitive structures (schemata, Gestalten, cell assemblies), thus categorizing and identifying the stimulus pattern, in a way commonly appropriate to reality confirmation. (b) In this process of structural assimilation some information is excluded, even though it registered. This excluded information is conjectured to have consequences of the same order as stimulus inputs registered without perception for any other reason. (c) Stimulus inputs unassimilated to structure may endure for some time in a state of readiness for assimilation to an available cognitive structure. The cognitive structures of fantasies are particularly available for assimilating this unstructured residue from stimulation; hence recovery in fantasy is to be expected.

The Freudian concepts of primary and secondary process are the best available conceptualizations of these processes, although there are related formulations from other sources. In any case, a full account of the processes of perception does well to consider the relationship between veridical perception and fantasy formation. In both cases events intervene between the stimulus and response that are not represented in awareness.

References

Adams, J. K. Laboratory studies of behavior without awareness. *Psychol. Rev.*, 1957, 54, 383-405.

Allers, R., & Teler, I. Über die unbemerkten Eindrücke bei Associatenen. *Z. Neurol. Psychiat.*, 1924, 89, 492-513. (Translated in *Psychol. Issues*, 1960, 2, Monogr. 7, 121-154.)

Bach, S. The symbolic effects of words in subliminal, supraliminal, and incidental presentation. Ph.D. dissertation, New York Univer., 1959.

Bagby, J. W. A cross-cultural study of perceptual predominance in binocular rivalry. *J. abnorm. soc. Psychol.*, 1957, 54, 331-334.

Blackwell, H. R. The influence of data collecting procedures upon psychophysical measurement of two sensory functions. *J. exp. Psychol.*, 1952, 44, 306-315.

Blackwell, H. R. Evaluation of the neural quantum theory in vision. *Amer. J. Psychol.*, 1953, 66, 397-408.

Bricker, D. P., & Chapanis, A. Do incorrectly perceived stimuli convey some information? *Psychol. Rev.*, 1953, 60, 181-188.

Bruner, J. S. Going beyond the information given. In Bruner, J. S., and others, *Contemporary approaches to cognition.* Cambridge, Mass.: Harvard Univer. Press, 1957, 41-69. (a)

Bruner, J. S. Neural mechanisms in perception. *Psychol. Rev.*, 1957, 64, 340-358. (b)

Cheatham, P. G. Visual perceptual latency as a function of stimulus brightness and contour shape. *J. exp. Psychol.*, 1952, 43, 369-380.

Davis, J. M. Personality, perceptual defense, and stereoscopic perception. *J. abnorm. soc. Psychol.*, 1959, 58, 398-402.

Eagle, M. The effects of subliminal stimuli of aggressive content upon conscious cognition. *J. Pers.* 1959, 27, 578-600.

Engel, E. The role of content in binocular resolution. *Amer. J. Psychol.*, 1956, 69, 87-91.

Eriksen, C. W. Discrimination and learning without awareness: A methodological survey and evaluation. *Psychol. Rev.*, 1960, 67, 279-300.

Fisher, C. Dreams and perception. *J. Amer. psychoanal. Assn.*, 1954, 3, 380-445.

Fisher, C. Dreams, images, and perception: A study of unconscious-preconscious relationships. *J. Amer. psychoanal. Assn.*, 1956, 4, 5-48.

Fisher, C. Subliminal and supraliminal influences on dreams. *Amer. J. Psychiat.*, 1960, 116, 1009-1017. (a)

Fisher, C. Introduction. In O. Poetzl and others. Preconscious stimulation in dreams, associations, and images. *Psychol. Issues*, 1960, 2, Monogr. 7, 1-40. (b)

Fisher, C., & Paul, I. H. The effect of subliminal visual stimulation on images and dreams: A validation study. *J. Amer. psychoanal. Assn.*, 1959, 7, 35-83.

Flavell, J. H., & Draguns, J. A microgenetic approach to perception and thought. *Psychol. Bull.*, 1957, 54, 197-217.

Garner, W. R., Hake, H. W., & Eriksen, C. W. Operationism and the concept of perception. *Psychol. Rev.*, 1956, 63, 149-159.

Goldberg, F., & Fiss, H. Partial cues and the phenomenon of "discrimination without awareness." *Percept. Mot. Skills*, 1959, 9, 243-251.

Goldiamond, I. Indicators of perception: I. Subliminal perception, subception, unconscious perception: An analysis in terms of psychophysical indicator methodology. *Psychol. Bull.*, 1958, 55, 373-411.

Goldstein, M. J., & Barthol, R. P. Fantasy responses to subliminal stimuli. *J. abnorm. soc. Psychol.*, 1960, 60, 22-26.

Hastorf, A. H., & Myro, G. The effect of meaning on binocular rivalry. *Amer. J. Psychol.*, 1959, 72, 393-400.

Hilgard, E. R. *Unconscious processes and man's rationality.* Urbana, Ill.: Univer. of Illinois Press, 1958.

Hilgard, E. R. Impulsive vs. realistic thinking: An examination of the distinction between primary and secondary processes in thought. *Psychol. Bull.* (In press, 1962)

Johnson, H., & Eriksen, C. W. Preconscious perception: A re-examination of the Poetzl phenomenon. *J. abnorm. soc. Psychol.*, 1961, 62, 497-503.

Klein, G. S. On subliminal activation. *J. nerv. ment. Dis.*, 1959, 128, 293-301.

Klein, G. S., Spence, D. P., Holt, R. R., & Gourevitch, S. Cognition without awareness: Subliminal influences upon conscious thought. *J. abnorm. soc. Psychol.*, 1958, 57, 255-266.

Lawrence, D. H., & Coles, G. R. Accuracy of recognition with alternatives before and after the stimulus. *J. exp. Psychol.*, 1954, 47, 208-214.

Lowenfeld, J. Negative affect as a causal factor in the occurrence of repression, subception, and perceptual defense. *J. Pers.*, 1961, 29, 54-63.

Luborsky, L., & Shevrin, H. Dreams and day-residues: A study of the Poetzl observation. *Bull. Menninger Clin.*, 1956, 20, 135-148.

Malamud, W., & Linder, F. E. Dreams and their relationship to recent impressions. *Arch. Neurol. Psychiat.*, 1931, 25, 1081-1099.

Paul, I. H., & Fisher, C. Subliminal visual stimulation: A study of its influence on subsequent images and dreams. *J. nerv. ment. Dis.*, 1959, 129, 315-340.

Pettigrew, T. V., Allport, G. W., & Barnett, E. O. Binocular resolution and perception of race in South Africa. *Brit. J. Psychol.*, 1958, 49, 265-278.

Pine, F. Incidental stimulation: A study of preconscious transformations. *J. abnorm. soc. Psychol.*, 1960, 60, 68-75.

Poetzl, O. Experimentell erregte Traumbilder in ihren Beziehungen zum indirekten Sehen. *Z. ges. Neurol. Psychiat.*, 1917, 37, 278-349. (Translated in *Psychol. Issues*, 1960, 3, Monogr. 7, 41-120.)

Rapaport, D. Consciousness: A psychopathological and psychodynamic view. In *Problems of consciousness*. Transactions of Second Conference, Josiah Macy, Jr., Foundtn., 1951, 18-57.

Rapaport, D. Cognitive structures. In J. S. Bruner and others, *Contemporary approaches to cognition*. Cambridge, Mass.: Harvard Univer. Press, 1957.

Russell, W. A., & Jenkins, J. J. The complete Minnesota norms for responses to 100 words from the Kent-Rosanoff Word Association Test. Minneapolis, Minn.: The Role of Language in Behavior, Tech. Report No. 11, 1954.

Shevrin, H., & Luborsky, L.   The measurement of preconscious perception
    in dreams and images: An investigation of the Poetzl phenomenon.
    J. abnorm. soc. Psychol., 1958, 56, 285-294.
Smith, G.   Visual perception: An event over time.   *Psychol. Rev.,* 1957,
    64, 306-313.
Smith, G., & Henriksson, M.   The effect on an established percept of a
    perceptual process beyond awareness.   *Acta Psychol.,* 1955, 11, 346-
    355.
Smith, G., Spence, D. P., & Klein, G. S.   Subliminal effects of verbal stimuli.
    J. abnorm. soc. Psychol., 1959, 59, 167-176.
Spence, D. P.   The multiple effects of subliminal stimuli.   *J. Pers.,* 1961,
    29, 40-53.
Swets, J. A.   Is there a sensory threshold?   *Science,* 1961, 134, 168-177.
Werner, H.   Studies on contour: I. Qualitative analysis.   *Amer. J. Psychol.,*
    1935, 47, 40-46.

The role of awareness in verbal conditioning

Charles D. Spielberger, *Duke University*

The successful utilization of operant-conditioning procedures to modify verbal behavior has been demonstrated most convincingly in a number of recent investigations (see reviews by Krasner, 1958; Salzinger, 1959). In verbal-conditioning studies, the subjects typically are instructed only to emit verbal behavior and the experimenter employs interpersonal stimuli such as "good" or "mmmhmm" to reinforce some preselected verbal response class. Increments in this reinforced response class for subjects judged to be unaware of any relationship between their own behavior and the experimenter's reinforcement have been interpreted as providing evidence that learning has occurred without awareness. Such evidence was reported in 29 of 31 verbal-conditioning studies reviewed by Krasner (1958). Although the results obtained in verbal-conditioning studies are remarkably consistent, the validity of the interpretation that the empirical findings provide evidence of learning without awareness requires further analysis of the concepts of learning and awareness as employed in these studies.

The principal objective in this paper is to examine the role of awareness in verbal conditioning. But before proceeding to this task, it will be useful first to consider some general factors in the climate of opinion in which psychologists interested in verbal conditioning have worked, which may have influenced the interpretation of evidence that subjects learn without awareness. This will require at least brief reference to the methods by which awareness has been investigated and the manner in which learning and awareness have been defined. We will then be in a better position to indicate how we propose to employ these concepts in reporting the results of four investigations of the operant conditioning of verbal behavior which we have conducted over the past several years.

The investigation of awareness in verbal-conditioning studies

The conceptual framework for much of the research on verbal conditioning is provided by Skinner's (1957) approach to verbal behavior in which the importance of establishing functional relations between observable independent variables and a speaker's verbal responses is emphasized. In Skinner's formulations, little recourse is made to the awareness of the speaker, i.e., his thoughts and ideas, in explaining verbal behavior. Furthermore, as Dulany (1959) has noted, although Skinner recognizes the possible importance of private stimuli to which the speaker alone is able to respond, these are not given systematic scientific status as variables controlling verbal behavior. It seems, therefore, paradoxical for experimenters working within a Skinnerian framework to be concerned about whether learning occurs with or without awareness.

Since awareness has not been included as a systematic construct in the conceptual framework which has generated much of the verbal-conditioning research, it might be expected that there would be relatively little concern about the methods used to investigate awareness in verbal-conditioning experiments. Absence of awareness has been typically inferred on the basis of subjects' responses to brief postconditioning interviews given, frequently, after a series of interpolated extinction trials (e.g., Buss, Gerjuoy, & Zussman, 1958; Cohen, Kalish, Thurston, & Cohen, 1954; Greenspoon, 1955). When more intensive interviewing procedures have been utilized immediately following acquisition trials (Krasner, Weiss, & Ullman, 1959; Krieckhaus & Eriksen, 1960; Levin, 1961), more subjects are judged to be aware of a correct contingency between their own behavior and the reinforcing stimuli or of response-reinforcement contingencies (correlated hypotheses) which bring partial reinforcement (Dulany, 1961; Tatz, 1960). It seems likely that experiments within the Skinnerian framework which have contended that verbal conditioning occurs without awareness may have been markedly influenced by implicit epistemological and methodological biases of which the investigators have not been aware.

The definition of learning in verbal-conditioning studies

In verbal-conditioning studies, the conclusion that learning has taken place is usually based on observed increments in the

rate of emission of some reinforced response class. Although it
is necessary to infer "what is learned" from subjects' responses
(Kendler, 1952), the implicit assumption that "emission of the
reinforced response class" is "what is learned" would preclude consideration of the possibility that learning can occur in the absence
of immediate effects upon performance. In contrast, a cognitive
learning theory might assume that awareness of a correct contingency is "what is learned" in verbal-conditioning experiments.
Here Campbell's (1954) argument that different learning theories
imply different operational definitions of the learned response is
particularly cogent.

In order to evaluate the role of awareness in verbal conditioning, a definition of learning which distinguishes between performance and learning, and which is at least neutral with respect
to the acceptance of awareness as a variable, would seem to be
required. Kimble's definition of learning (1961, pp. 2-8) as "a
relatively permanent change in behavior *potentiality* which occurs
as a result of reinforced practice" would seem particularly appropriate. According to this definition learning may be inferred
from behavior which occurs some time after the potential to produce the behavior was acquired, as well as from behavior which
occurs concomitantly with or immediately following reinforced
practice. In order to conclude that learning has occurred in cases
where the appearance of what is learned in behavioral change is
not immediate, it would be necessary for the subject to specify
verbally the behavior that could be performed if he chose to do so.
To illustrate with an example from Kimble, suppose that one
examines a road map and then drives directly to a distant city. If
we assume that the act of driving to this city would have been
impossible without consulting the map, the successful completion of
the trip clearly depends upon previous practice with the map.
Learning in this case could be ascertained by the actual performance of the travel, or by operations which required the subject
to indicate his awareness of a correct route. A more complete
delineation of what was learned would be provided by a combina-
tion of both types of operations.

If we accept a concept of learning defined in terms of behavior
potentiality, the operations for delineating what is learned in verbal-
conditioning experiments may be in terms of performance, or

awareness (verbal reports), or both. We may now turn to the concept of awareness.

The concept of awareness

The import of awareness or immediate experience for the science of psychology, historically, has raised many epistemological, theoretical, and methodological issues. Some psychologists consider the indices or operational criteria for awareness as the only meaning that can be given legitimately to the term; others have used awareness as a construct based upon such indices but without implication of any experiential referent. But, as Adams (1957) has noted, in the latter definition the clarity gained by introducing awareness as a response-defined intervening variable in order to avoid phenomenological meaning is more apparent than real. For this definition reduces to the first and thereby limits the meaning of awareness to the particular indices employed.

In the present context, awareness will be regarded as a process which intervenes between stimuli and responses whose properties may be delimited by converging operations. The concept of awareness proposed here is analogous in its definitional properties to the concept of perception suggested by Garner, Hake, and Eriksen (1956). Although the *scientific* meaning of awareness is considered to reside exclusively in the operations performed which converge upon the concept, it seems imperative that one also state his *prescientific* assumptions about concepts such as awareness in order to provide others with a better understanding of the particular choice of converging operations. Awareness in the present context will refer in a general way to the conscious experiences (thoughts, ideas, and hypotheses) of the subjects in our verbal-conditioning experiments.

The proposed usage of awareness as a concept implies systematic scientific status for processes that are not directly observable by the experimenter and which have variously been referred to as immediate experience, direct experience, or phenomenal experience (Zener, 1958). In recognizing the significance of phenomenal experience for the science of psychology, we also accept the responsibility for attempting to deal with the complex technical problems which arise in specifying relations between awareness and the verbal reports from which it is usually inferred in psychological experiments. With regard to verbal reports, Eriksen (1958, 1960) has indicated inherent limitations in too exclusive a dependence upon operations which infer awareness from verbal responses to interview questions. Such operations run the dual risk of either failing to detect awareness when the interview questions are brief and general or suggesting awareness when the questions are detailed and specific. It will be contended in this paper that, because of insensitive interviewing procedures, failure to detect awareness has contributed to the positive results obtained in many investigations of verbal conditioning which have purported to demonstrate learning without awareness. And even though it may not be possible to avoid suggesting awareness to some subjects when detailed postconditioning interviews are used, we will contend that such interviews are to be preferred to the superficial interviews generally employed in investigations of the operant conditioning of verbal behavior. These contentions will be supported by experiments to which we may now turn.

Experiments on the operant conditioning of verbal behavior

In the four experiments to be reported, a sentence-construction task devised by Taffel (1955) was employed as the operant-conditioning procedure. The stimulus materials for the conditioning task consisted of 3 × 5-inch white index cards on each of which a different past-tense verb was typed. Below the verb the pronouns "I," "we," "you," "he," "she," and "they" were typed in different sequences. In all four experiments the reinforced response class was first-person pronouns and the reinforcing stimulus was the experimenter's saying "good." The subjects were tested individually; they were instructed to make up a sentence for each card beginning with one of the pronouns and containing the verb. Each sentence was defined as a trial and was recorded verbatim by the experimenter. The first 20 trials were not reinforced so that the subjects' level of free operant responding with "I, we" sentences could be determined.

Awareness was inferred from subjects' responses to a lengthy postconditioning interview[1] (PCI) conducted immediately following acquisition trials. A subject was considered to be aware if he stated that "good" had followed sentences beginning with "I"

[1] The PCI employed in Experiments I and II is given in Levin (1961).

alone, with "we" alone, or with "I" or "we." These contingencies if acted upon would bring 100 per cent reinforcement. A further requirement was that the subject indicate in response to a PCI question that he had been aware of the contingency during the conditioning trials.

Experiment I: Awareness and verbal conditioning.

In the first experiment Levin (1961) investigated the possibility that previous findings which have reported operant conditioning of verbal behavior without awareness might be artifacts of insensitive interviewing procedures. The subjects, male hospitalized medical and neuropsychiatric patients, were randomly assigned to a systematically reinforced and a nonreinforced group. The subjects were given 20 nonreinforced (free operant) trials followed by 80 conditioning trials; they were interviewed immediately subsequent to the final conditioning trial. The first four questions of the PCI, hereafter referred to as the Brief Interview (BI), approximated those typically used to determine awareness in other verbal-conditioning experiments (e.g., Cohen *et al.,* 1954; Taffel, 1955). The remaining questions, hereafter referred to as the Extended Interview (EI), were designed to elicit additional information about subjects' awareness during the conditioning trials while not suggesting a correct contingency to them.

Only 3 of 60 reinforced subjects were determined to be aware on the basis of their responses to the BI. The data for these subjects were excluded from further consideration as is the custom in verbal-conditioning investigations. The conditioning data for the remaining subjects who received reinforcement and for the nonreinforced controls, grouped into blocks of 20 trials, are depicted in Figure 1A. These findings suggested that when awareness was inferred on the basis of responses to the BI, unaware subjects learned.[2] But when the EI was employed as the basis for inferring awareness, the evidence for conditioning without awareness was found to be largely accounted for by 16 subjects who failed to verbalize awareness in response to the BI but who did so during the EI. The conditioning data for the 16 aware subjects are compared in Figure 1B with the performance of the reinforced

[2] All findings referred to in the text of the paper were significant at or beyond the .05 level of confidence unless it is specifically stated otherwise.

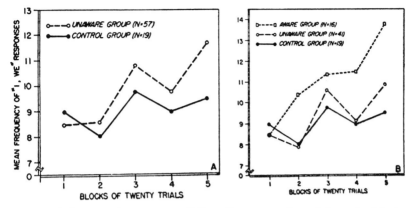

Figure 1 (A). Mean frequencies of "I, we" sentences for reinforced subjects classified as unaware on the basis of their responses to a brief interview and for nonreinforced controls; (B) Mean frequencies of "I, we" sentences for subjects classified as aware on the basis of their responses to the extended interview, for subjects classified as unaware on the basis of their responses to the extended interview, and for controls.

subjects who were unaware of a response-reinforcement contingency.[3]

Although first-person pronouns were reinforced for all subjects, only 6 of the 16 subjects who verbalized awareness during the EI indicated that they were aware that sentences beginning with both "I" and "we" were reinforced. Eight subjects stated that the reinforcer followed sentences beginning with "I" while 2 subjects said that it had followed sentences beginning with "we." The data for the latter 10 subjects were evaluated in order to determine whether they responded differentially to the reinforced pronoun for which they were aware of a contingency (RP-A) as compared to the reinforced pronoun for which they were unaware of a contingency (RP-U), and to determine whether or not conditioning without awareness occurred for the RP-U. It may be noted in

[3] Although the unaware subjects did not, as a group, show evidence of conditioning, a small subgroup of them who were unaware of the "Good" in addition to being unaware of a correct response-reinforcement contingency showed significant improvement in performance on the conditioning task (Levin, 1961). This finding would be consistent with the hypothesis that these subjects learned without awareness. But these subjects were less adequately interviewed than other subjects in the study since the interview was terminated midway through the EI when they failed to indicate that they were aware that the experimenter had occasionally said "Good." More intensive interviewing may have revealed some of these subjects to be aware of a response-reinforcement contingency.

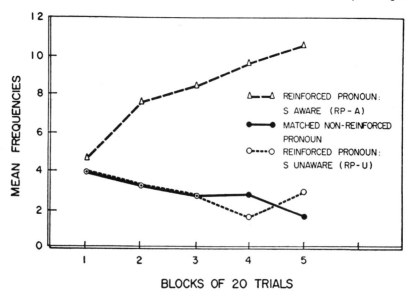

Figure 2. Mean frequencies for the reinforced pronoun for which subjects were aware of a response-reinforcement contingency (RP-A), for the reinforced pronoun for which subjects were unaware of a correct contingency (RP-U), and for a nonreinforced pronoun matched with the RP-U on initial operant level.

Figure 2 that the number of sentences beginning with the RP-A increased markedly over trials while the number of sentences beginning with the RP-U declined at about the same rate as a nonreinforced pronoun matched with it for free operant level.

The findings would seem to contradict the assertion that verbal conditioning provides a "clear example of direct, automatic, or in other words, unconscious learning" (Dollard & Miller, 1950, p. 44). The fact that subjects' performance was specific to the pronouns of which they were aware of a correct response-reinforcement contingency rather than those that were reinforced is consistent with the hypothesis that awareness of a correct contingency mediated performance. If reinforcement automatically and unconsciously strengthened reinforced responses, then the rate of emission of both the RP-A and the RP-U would have been expected to increase.

It would seem reasonable to assume that the intensive PCI employed in this investigation reduced the probability that aware subjects went undetected. However, the additional cues provided by the EI undoubtedly increased the probability that awareness may have been suggested during the PCI to some subjects who had not been aware during the conditioning trials. But even if this were the case, the operational definition of awareness in terms of the EI was more useful than awareness defined on the basis of responses to the BI. The fact that subjects who verbalized awareness acquired the conditioned response while the unaware subjects as a group did not suggests that in order to account for a larger proportion of the total variance in verbal-conditioning studies, intensive interviews should be employed. Furthermore, verbalization of awareness would appear to be an important empirical variable in verbal conditioning, irrespective of whether subjects' verbalizations indicate awareness during the conditioning task or the effects of suggestion by cues in the PCI. However, the possibility of the second alternative complicates the evaluation of the relationship between awareness and behavior in this study. The question concerning the relationship between awareness and performance may be restated as follows: Was it the subject's awareness during the experiment which mediated his performance? Or, was awareness suggested during the PCI to subjects who showed increments in performance during the conditioning trials? Evidence bearing on these alternatives will be provided in the following experiments.

Experiment II: Awareness, attitude toward the reinforcement and verbal conditioning[4]

It has been tacitly assumed in most verbal-conditioning studies that reinforcing stimuli such as "good" and "mmmhmm" are "generalized conditioned reinforcers" (Skinner, 1957, pp. 53-54) which have essentially the same reinforcing properties for all subjects. Evidence that this assumption may not be tenable has been reported by Mandler and Kaplan (1956) who found that the reinforcing stimulus "mmmhmm" operated to produce an increment in performance for subjects who subjectively evaluated it as positive,

[4] The research reported in Experiments II, III, and IV was supported in part by a grant from the National Institute of Mental Health (OM-362). The technical and clerical assistance of Larilee Baty, Edna Bissette, J. B. Grier, and Kay Howard in processing the data are acknowledged with appreciation. The author is particularly indebted to S. M. Levin for his collaboration in Experiments II and III.

while the same stimulus produced a decrement in performance for subjects who regarded it as a negative stimulus. The second study in this series (Spielberger, Levin, & Shepard, 1962) was designed to examine the effects of awareness on verbal conditioning when the subject's attitude toward the reinforcement was taken into account. The stimulus materials, the procedure, and the PCI in this experiment were the same as those employed in Experiment I. The subjects were 45 undergraduate female liberal arts students.

The effects of awareness on conditioning. Of the 30 reinforced subjects, 19 were determined to be aware of a correct response-reinforcement contingency. The performance of the 13 subjects who were determined to be aware on the basis of their responses to the BI (Aware-BI) and the 6 subjects who verbalized their awareness to the EI (Aware-EI) are compared with unaware and control subjects in Figure 3A. The aware groups demonstrated a greater rate of acquisition of the conditioned-response class than did Unaware and Control groups. Furthermore, it may be noted in Figure 3B that, as was the case in Experiment I, when

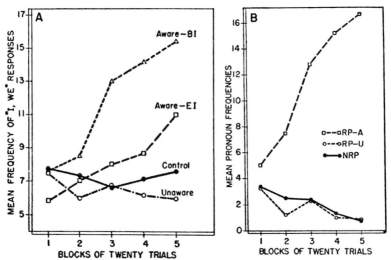

Figure 3 (A). Mean frequencies of "I, we" sentences for Aware-BI, Aware-EI, Unaware, and Control groups; *(B)* Mean frequencies for the reinforced pronoun for which subjects were aware of a response-reinforcement contingency (RP-A), for the reinforced pronoun for which subjects were unaware of a correct contingency (RP-U), and for a nonreinforced pronoun (NRP) matched with the RP-U for free operant level.

subjects were aware of a response-reinforcement contingency for only one of the reinforced pronouns (RP-A), improvement in performance was specific to that pronoun. There was no evidence of learning for the reinforced pronoun (RP-U) of which subjects were unaware of a response-reinforcement contingency since the performance on the RP-U was comparable to the emission of a nonreinforced pronoun (NRP) matched with it for initial operant level. When the conditioning data for individual subjects were examined, it was found that not a single unaware subject showed an increment in the frequency of "I, we" sentences from Trial Block 1 to Trial Block 5 of more than one such response.

The effects of attitude toward reinforcement on conditioning. Attitude toward the reinforcement was determined from subjects' responses to the PCI question: "Would you say you wanted me to say 'Good'?" The question was initially presented in open-ended form but the subjects were subsequently required to choose from among three alternatives: "very much"; "some"; "didn't care one way or the other." Since none of the unaware subjects showed acquisition of the conditioned-response class, only aware subjects were included in the analysis of the effects of attitude toward the reinforcement on conditioning. On the basis of their responses to the forced-choice form of the question, the 19 aware subjects were assigned to three groups which were assumed to differ in their desire to receive the reinforcement. These groups were designated Aware-VM, Aware-S, and Aware-DC and consisted of 4, 6, and 9 subjects, respectively.

The response measure employed for each subject in the analysis of the conditioning data was the specific pronoun or pronouns for which the subject was aware of a correct response-reinforcement contingency. Using this measure, however, introduced greater individual differences in subjects' free operant level for the first block of trials. In order to control for such variability, difference scores were employed. These were derived for each subject by subtracting the frequency of sentences in the free operant block of trials which began with the pronoun or pronouns for which the subject was aware of a correct contingency from the frequency of such sentences in the four subsequent blocks of conditioning trials. The mean difference scores for the Aware-VM, the Aware-S, and the Aware-DC groups are compared in Figure 4 with mean difference scores computed for the Unaware and Control groups. Those subjects who stated that they wanted very much to receive the reinforcement showed a significantly greater rate of acquisition of the pronoun or pronouns for which they were aware of a correct contingency than did subjects with less positive attitudes toward the reinforcement. Although the difference between the Aware-S and Aware-DC groups was not statistically significant, both significantly exceeded the Unaware and Control groups in the acquisition of reinforced responses.

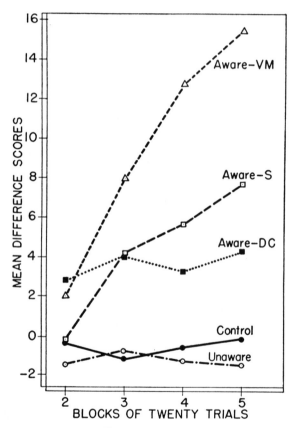

Figure 4. Mean difference scores for "I, we" sentences for aware subjects who indicated "very much," "some," or "don't care" attitudes toward the reinforcement compared with mean difference scores for the Unaware and Control groups.

Before proceeding to the next experiment, the principal findings of Experiment II may be summarized briefly: (*a*) subjects aware of a correct response-reinforcement contingency showed significant acquisition of the conditioned-response class; (*b*) subjects unaware of a correct response-reinforcement contingency showed no increments in conditioning performance; (*c*) the performance on the conditioning task of aware subjects was specific to the pronoun or pronouns for which they were aware of a correct contingency; (*d*) the performance of aware subjects was also related to the subjects' attitude toward the reinforcement. The possibility, however, that awareness was suggested by the interview could not be ruled out, especially for the 6 subjects in this study who verbalized their awareness during the EI.

Experiment III: The effects of instructions on awareness and performance in verbal conditioning

Our third verbal-conditioning study had four major objectives: (*a*) to evaluate the effects of instructions on awareness and attitude toward the reinforcement; (*b*) to determine the effects of instructions and awareness on conditioning; (*c*) to examine the conditioning data of aware subjects to determine if the increments in their performance on the conditioning task coincided with the trial block on which they stated that they became aware; and (*d*) to evaluate the possibility that a correct response-reinforcement contingency might be suggested to subjects during the PCI. This experiment differed from Experiments I and II in that 100 reinforced trials were employed rather than 80, instructions were manipulated, and there were two experimenters. One experimenter ran the conditioning trials and a second experimenter conducted the PCI. The subjects were 48 female student nurses.

The PCI was modified[5] on the basis of our experience with it in the two previous experiments. The modification of the PCI consisted of eliminating questions in the EI which had not contributed to the determination of subjects' awareness in Experiments I and II and adding a confrontation question for subjects who had not verbalized a correct contingency by the end of the

[5] We are indebted to K. Zener for his invaluable aid in modifying the interview and for suggesting the inclusion of the confrontation question. The modified PCI used in Experiments III and IV is shown in Table 1.

EI. The questions for determining awareness in the modified PCI are presented in Table 1.

The effects of instructions on awareness and attitude toward reinforcement. Neutral and learning instructions were employed. The neutral instructions were essentially the same as those used in Experiment I. The subjects given learning instructions were told that a certain technique for constructing sentences would be considered correct. It has been demonstrated that a set to look for a principle facilitated both awareness and learning on a task involving verbal reinforcement (DiVesta & Blake, 1959).

Instructions had the expected effects on awareness. Of the 20 subjects given learning instructions, 15 were aware; all of these subjects verbalized awareness of the response-reinforcement contingency to the BI. Of the 20 subjects given neutral instructions, 13 were aware; 9 of them verbalized awareness to the BI and 4 to the EI. When the effects of instructions on attitude toward the

Table 1. Postconditioning interview for awareness.[a]

I'd like to ask you some questions about the experiment you were just in. In answering these questions, it is important that you think back to when you were going through the cards.

1. Did you usually give the first sentence that came to your mind?
2. How did you go about deciding which of the words to use?
3. Did you think you were using some words more often than others? Which words? Why?
4. What did you think the purpose of this was?
5. While going through the cards did you think that you were supposed to make up your sentences in any particular way, or that you were supposed to change the way in which you made up your sentences? How?
6. Did you notice anything about the experimenter while you were going through the cards?
7. Did you notice that she said anything?
8. Actually she did occasionally say "good." Thinking back now to when you were going through the cards, do you remember her saying "good"?
9. (Thinking back now to when you were going through the cards) What did her saying "good" mean to you?
10. Did you try to figure out what made her say "good" or why or when she was saying "good"?
11. What ideas did you have about what was making her say "good"?
12. While going through the cards, did you think that her saying "good" had anything to do with the words you chose to begin your sentences? What?
13. Did you ever have the idea that she was saying "good" after sentences beginning with *he* or *she*? *I* or *we*?

[a] Questions 1 through 4 comprised the BI, Questions 5-12 the EI, and Question 13 served as the confrontation question. The awareness portion of the PCI was terminated if a subject verbalized a correct response-reinforcement contingency. For subjects who spontaneously verbalized awareness of the "good" prior to Question 7, Questions 7 and 8 were omitted. The above questions were designed to elicit information regarding subjects' awareness. Additional PCI questions asked subsequent to the above inquired about subjects' attitudes toward the reinforcing stimuli and elicited statements from aware subjects as to the trial block on which they became aware of a response-reinforcement contingency.

reinforcement were examined, it was found that 85 per cent of the subjects given learning instructions wanted "very much" or "some" to receive the reinforcement as compared to 70 per cent of the subjects given neutral instructions. Stated differently, of the 9 subjects who indicated they "didn't care" about the reinforcement, 6 had received neutral instructions.

The effects of instructions and awareness on conditioning. Since it was demonstrated in Experiments I and II that subjects who were aware of a correct response-reinforcement contingency for only one of the reinforced pronouns showed conditioning specific to that pronoun, the response measures employed in the analysis of the conditioning data in Experiment III were the pronoun ("I" or "we") or pronouns ("I" and "we") of which each subject was aware of a correct contingency. As in Experiment II, difference scores were computed to reduce individual variability. Difference scores were derived by subtracting the frequency of sentences in Trial Block 1 beginning with the pronoun or pronouns of which each subject was aware from the frequency of such sentences in the subsequent five blocks of conditioning trials.

The conditioning curves of subjects given learning instructions who were aware of a correct response-reinforcement contingency (Aware-L) and subjects given these instructions who were unaware of a correct contingency (Unaware-L) are compared in Figure 5A with the conditioning curves of subjects given neutral instructions who were aware (Aware-N) or unaware (Unaware-N) of a correct contingency. The Aware-L group showed the greatest increment in performance on the conditioning task. It was evident that, by Trial Block 6, most of the subjects in this group were performing at near-asymptotic levels. On the final trial block, the mean frequency of "I, we" sentences for the Aware-L group was 19.1. Examination of the conditioning data for individual subjects in the Aware-L group revealed that 12 of the 15 subjects began all of their sentences in Trial Block 6 with the pronoun or pronouns for which they were aware of a correct contingency. The performance curve for the Unaware-L group was similar to that of the controls.

It may be noted in Figure 5A that the performance curves for the subjects given neutral instructions fall between those for subjects given learning instructions. Furthermore, the Aware-N and

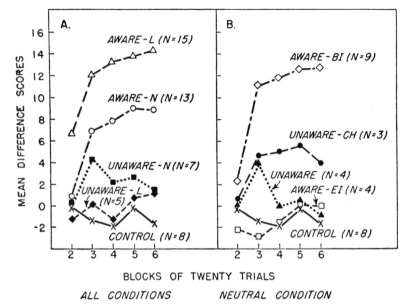

BLOCKS OF TWENTY TRIALS

ALL CONDITIONS   NEUTRAL CONDITION

Figure 5 (A). Mean difference scores for "I, we" sentences for subjects given learning instructions who were aware (Aware-L) or unaware (Unaware-L) of a response-reinforcement contingency, and for subjects given neutral instructions who were aware (Aware-N) or unaware (Unaware-N) of a correct contingency compared to mean difference scores for the Control group; (B) Mean difference scores for subjects given neutral instructions who verbalized their awareness to the brief interview (Aware-BI), and to the extended interview (Aware-EI), for subjects who, although unaware of a correct contingency, had correlated hypotheses (Unaware-CH), for subjects who were unaware and had no correlated hypotheses (Unaware), and for the Control group.

Unaware-N groups showed much greater variability than the comparable groups given learning instructions. Therefore, a more detailed analysis of the conditioning data for these groups was undertaken to determine if some of the variance could be accounted for by factors related to subjects' awareness. First, the interview responses of the 7 subjects in the Unaware-N group were evaluated by two raters who had no knowledge of the conditioning data. Three subjects were reliably judged (complete agreement) to have correlated hypotheses which would bring partial reinforcement: one thought that "I" and "he" were reinforced; the second thought that she was supposed to tell stories about herself and the third believed that she was supposed to make up sentences about her school experiences. It may be noted in Figure 5B that unaware subjects with correlated hypotheses (Unaware-CH) showed some improvement in performance on the conditioning task while the conditioning curve of totally unaware subjects (Unaware) was more similar to that of the controls.

The Aware-N group was also divided into two subgroups on the basis of whether these subjects verbalized their awareness to the BI or to the EI; the groups were designated Aware-BI and Aware-EI, respectively. It may be noted in Figure 5B that the Aware-BI group performed at about the same level as aware subjects given learning instructions (see Figure 5A). The Aware-EI group did not show any performance increment. The possibility that awareness was suggested to subjects in the Aware-EI group will be considered in a later section.

The relationship between attitude toward the reinforcement and conditioning was essentially the same as that found in Experiment II (see Figure 4). Those subjects who wanted the reinforcement "very much" demonstrated the highest degree of acquisition of the reinforced responses. Of the 13 aware subjects who wanted the reinforcement "very much," 12 began *all* of their sentences in the final trial block with the pronoun or pronouns for which they were aware of a correct contingency. Of the 13 aware subjects who wanted the reinforcement "very much," 9 had received learning instructions. Thus, learning instructions caused more subjects to be aware and to want the reinforcement "very much," and aware subjects who very much wanted the reinforcement showed the highest level of acquisition of the reinforced responses.

Increments in conditioning performance as a function of the trial block on which subjects stated that they became aware of a response-reinforcement contingency. At the end of the PCI, all aware subjects were asked to indicate on which trial block during the conditioning trials they became aware of the response-reinforcement contingency. They were told that there had been 100 cards (trials) subsequent to the practice (free operant) period and were asked: "Would you say that idea (about the response-reinforcement contingency) occurred to you during the first 20 cards; the second 20 cards; the third; the fourth; or the fifth?"

This question provided a converging operation for evaluating another aspect of the subjects' awareness and permitted analysis of conditioning performance as a function of the trial block on which subjects stated that they became aware. For this analysis, the data for aware subjects given neutral and learning instructions were combined. The 28 aware subjects were divided into three groups: the 16 subjects who indicated that they became aware during Trial Block 2 were designated the Aware-Bl 2 group; the 7 subjects who stated that they became aware during Trial Block 3 were designated the Aware-Bl 3 group; the 5 subjects who indicated that they became aware during Trial Blocks 4 and 5 were designated the Aware-Bl 4 group. All of the aware subjects indicated that they became aware prior to Trial Block 6.

The response measures for the analysis of the conditioning data were the difference scores derived for the analysis of the effects of instructions and awareness on conditioning. The mean difference scores for the Aware-Bl 2, the Aware-Bl 3, the Aware-Bl 4 and the Control groups are compared in Figure 6. Increments in performance on the conditioning task for the three groups of aware subjects tended to occur on the particular trial block during which these subjects stated in the PCI that they became aware of the response-reinforcement contingency. This finding is consistent with the hypothesis that subjects' awareness mediated their performance. A theory of automatic strengthening of response by reinforcement would predict a gradual increase in performance on the conditioning task as a function of reinforced practice.

The possibility that a response-reinforcement contingency was suggested in the interview. Suggestion in verbal-conditioning experiments could conceivably operate in at least two ways: (*a*) the experimenter who ran the subjects on the conditioning task would, consequently, have knowledge of the subjects' performance; the experimenter might differentially suggest hypotheses about the experiment during the PCI which corresponded to the subjects' performance on the conditioning task; or (*b*) the PCI questions might be leading and thereby provide cues which suggested hypotheses to subjects who were previously unaware. Fortunately, the first type of suggestion can be easily controlled by simply utilizing one experimenter for the conditioning task and a different

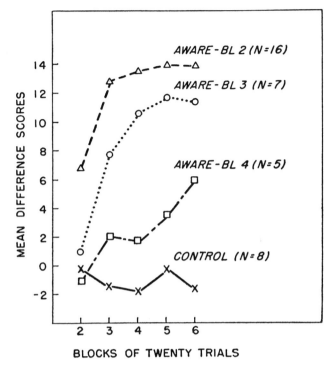

Figure 6. Mean difference scores for "I, we" sentences for aware subjects who stated during the postconditioning interview that they became aware during the second block of trials (Aware-Bl 2), the third block of trials (Aware-Bl 3), or during the fourth or fifth blocks of trials (Aware-Bl 4) compared to the conditioning performance of the Control group.

experimenter to conduct the interview. This procedure was employed in the present experiment.

The confrontation question which was added to the PCI attempted to get at the second form of suggestion. But, of the 12 unaware subjects who were confronted with a correct response-reinforcement contingency, none was found to be aware on the basis of her responses to the confrontation question. It was possible, however, that awareness had been suggested in this experiment to the four subjects given neutral instructions who verbalized their awareness to the EI and who failed to show any performance increment. All of these subjects verbalized awareness prior to the confrontation question; three of them indicated "some" desire for the experimenter to say "Good." For these three subjects, it would appear that their verbal reports concerning their awareness during the conditioning trials were unreliable, or their statements about their attitudes toward the reinforcement were unreliable, or both. In order to explore further the possibility that awareness is suggested by cues provided by the PCI, the final study to be reported focused centrally upon this question.

Experiment IV: Confrontation and the possibility of suggesting a response-reinforcement contingency in verbal conditioning

The primary aim in this study (Church, 1961) was to evaluate the effects on conditioning of directly confronting subjects with a response-reinforcement contingency. The procedure employed utilized neutral instructions, 80 reinforced trials, and the modified PCI employed in Experiment III which included the confrontation question. All subjects who at the end of the EI had not verbalized awareness were confronted with a correct response-reinforcement contingency. The subjects were 30 female undergraduate students.

Of the 20 subjects who received reinforcement, 18 stated that they had been aware of a response-reinforcement contingency during the conditioning trials. Since the purpose of the experiment was to evaluate the possibility that a correct contingency was suggested during the PCI, the two unaware subjects were eliminated from further consideration. The 18 subjects who stated that they became aware of a response-reinforcement contingency during the conditioning trials were divided into three groups on the basis of the interview question to which they verbalized awareness: 7 subjects verbalized awareness to the BI (Aware-BI); 5 to the EI excluding the confrontation question (Aware-EI); and 6 to the confrontation question (Aware-C). The performances of these three groups are compared with that of the Control group in Figure 7. Difference scores, derived as in Experiment III and based on the pronoun or pronouns for which individual subjects were aware of response-reinforcement contingencies, were the response measures in the analysis of the conditioning data. As in Experiments II and III, the Aware-BI group showed greater acquisition of the reinforced responses than the Aware-EI group. The latter group showed a higher degree of acquisition of the reinforced responses than subjects in the Aware-C group. The per-

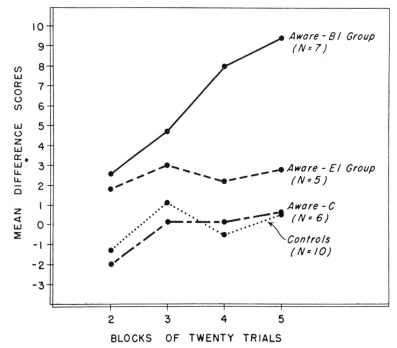

Figure 7. Mean difference scores for "I, we" sentences for subjects who verbalized awareness to the brief interview (Aware-BI), to the extended interview excluding the confrontation question (Aware-EI), or to the confrontation question (Aware-C) compared to the Control group.

formance of the subjects who did not verbalize awareness until they were directly confronted with a correct response-reinforcement contingency was comparable to that of the Control group. The evaluation of the over-all differences between the four groups yielded an F which was statistically significant, but the F test of the difference between the Aware-EI and the Aware-C groups was not significant. Given the small Ns, the range of attitudes toward the reinforcement, which contributed additional variability to the Aware-EI group, and the possibility that awareness was suggested to some subjects in this group, the failure of this difference to reach a satisfactory level of statistical significance was not altogether surprising.

It seemed probable that awareness had been suggested to the 6 subjects who indicated their awareness of a response-reinforcement contingency to the confrontation question. The failure of these subjects to show an increment in performance could not be accounted for by indifferent attitudes toward the reinforcement in that 4 of them indicated "some" desire to receive the reinforcement. As an independent estimate of the awareness of subjects in this experiment, the interviewer, who had no knowledge of the subjects' performance on the conditioning task, assessed the subjects' awareness on the basis of their responses to the PCI. Five subjects were judged to have had awareness suggested to them during the PCI. All five subjects had verbalized their awareness to the confrontation question.

The role of awareness in verbal conditioning

In order to examine implications for the role of awareness in verbal conditioning of the experiments reported in this paper, it will be useful beforehand to review the aggregate findings of the four studies: (a) It was clearly demonstrated that verbal behavior could be modified by reinforcing selected classes of emitted verbal responses. (b) Acquisition of the reinforced response class was observed for "unaware" subjects when brief interviews were employed as the operations for determining awareness. (c) There was no evidence of learning without awareness, except possibly in Experiment I (see Footnote 3), when extended interviews were employed to infer awareness. (d) The acquisition of the reinforced responses by aware subjects was specific to the pronoun or pronouns for which these subjects were aware of a correct response-reinforcement contingency. (e) Increments in the conditioning curves of aware subjects corresponded to the trial block on which they stated during the postconditioning interview that they became aware. (f) Subjects who verbalized awareness in response to direct confrontation with a correct contingency in the postconditioning interview did not manifest increments in performance on the conditioning task. (g) Learning instructions increased the number of subjects who became aware of a response-reinforcement contingency and the readiness with which these subjects verbalized their awareness. (h) Learning instructions also tended to induce more positive attitudes toward the reinforcement. (i) Subjects with the most positive attitudes toward the reinforcement showed the greatest acquisition of the reinforced responses.

What conclusions may be drawn from these findings about the role of awareness in verbal conditioning? Given the concepts of learning and awareness proposed earlier, the data suggest that "what is learned" in verbal-conditioning experiments is awareness of a response-reinforcement contingency which may be acted upon if the subject desires to receive the reinforcement. This interpretation is suggested most clearly by the finding, in all four experiments, that conditioning was specific to the pronoun or pronouns for which the subjects were aware of a contingency rather than the pronouns which were reinforced. The interpretation is supported by the findings in Experiments II, III, and IV that only aware subjects learned, and that those aware subjects who wanted most to receive the reinforcement showed the greatest degree of acquisition of the reinforced responses. Thus, awareness of a response-reinforcement contingency would appear to be a necessary condition for the acquisition (increase in the rate of emission) of a reinforced response, and the extent to which aware subjects act on what they learn would seem to depend upon how much they want to receive the reinforcement.

Theoretical interpretations of the findings

The empirical findings of verbal-conditioning studies have been cited as evidence of the appropriateness of Skinner's descriptive behaviorism as an approach to the understanding of verbal behavior (Salzinger, 1959). We have found, however, that the framework of cognitive-learning theory is more useful for generating hypotheses and explaining results in verbal-conditioning experiments. The latter point of view suggested specific hypotheses which led to the observation in our data of previously unreported relationships between performance on the conditioning task and (a) awareness of a correct response-reinforcement contingency for a single reinforced pronoun, and (b) awareness of the particular trial block of the conditioning task on which subjects stated, during the postconditioning interview, that they first became aware of a correct contingency. It is unlikely that these relationships would have been predicted by a theoretical approach to verbal behavior which denies phenomenal experience (awareness) systematic status.

The results of verbal-conditioning studies, including those reported in the present paper, can, of course, be interpreted in other terms. Most investigators working with verbal conditioning have ascribed the effects on performance of their conditioning procedures to the reinforcing stimuli administered by the experimenter. A recent analysis of verbal conditioning offered by Skinner[6] has involved the assumption that the "Good" is a discriminative stimulus rather than a reinforcement. The successful conditioning of some response classes and the failure to condition others (and presumably the fact that some subjects condition and others do not) is then explained in terms of the subject's prior conditioning history with respect to audience variables. Although awareness as a systematic construct is thereby avoided, this interpretation would appear to place considerable burden upon the experimenter for verification of the subject's prior conditioning history.

The findings of verbal-conditioning studies have been cited as demonstrating "that the effects of a reinforcement can be entirely unconscious and automatic" (Dollard & Miller, 1950, p. 44). Interpretation of the findings of Experiments II, III, and IV in these terms would encounter difficulty in accounting for the fact that conditioning was specific to the pronouns for which subjects were aware of a correct response-reinforcement contingency rather than those pronouns that were reinforced, as well as for the more general failure of the reinforcement to have the expected effects upon the performance of unaware subjects. In addition, a number of assumptions about aware subjects who showed improved performance on the conditioning task would appear to be required of those who wish to maintain this view; it would be necessary to assume: (a) that awareness was suggested by the cues of the interview to some of the subjects who verbalized awareness; (b) that the subjects to whom awareness was suggested retrospectively recalled their performance and accurately described it in their verbal reports; and (c) that these subjects also verbalized attitudes toward the reinforcement so as to be consistent with their performance on the conditioning task. On the basis of data similar in many respects to that reported here, Dulany (1961) has recently concluded that "a theory of automatic strengthening by aftereffects apparently does not account for these [verbal-conditioning] findings without auxiliary assumptions or radical augmentation." This conclusion is strongly supported by our findings.

[6] Personal communication to Matarazzo, Saslow, and Pareis (1960, p. 205).

Regardless of one's theoretical orientation, one implication of the experiments presented here seems inescapable. Verbalization of awareness to intensive interview questions is an important empirical variable in investigations of verbal conditioning regardless of whether the subjects' verbal reports are interpreted as indicating awareness during the conditioning trials or awareness suggested by the cues of the postconditioning interview. The fact that more systematic variance was accounted for when the conditioning data were analyzed on the basis of responses to intensive interviews than when brief interviews were employed argues strongly for the potential explanatory gain from using intensive interviewing procedures not only in verbal-conditioning studies but, more generally, in psychological experiments with human subjects.

Experimental conditions which influence verbal conditioning

Other factors independent of theoretical orientation which would seem to be important in verbal-conditioning experiments are: (a) the characteristics of the subject populations on whom the experiments are conducted, (b) the instructions given the subjects, and (c) the nature of the verbal-conditioning procedure.

Characteristics of subjects. Much of the positive evidence for verbal conditioning without awareness comes from studies in which psychiatric patients were the subjects (e.g., Buss & Gerjuoy, 1958; Cohen *et al.,* 1954; Leventhal, 1959; Taffel, 1955). But since patient populations are generally comprised of relatively less intelligent, less sophisticated subjects with inadequate vocabularies and vague conceptual categories, for these subjects the relationship between awareness and learning is likely to be difficult to evaluate. Evidence for conditioning without awareness obtained in experiments in which patients served as subjects would appear to be suspect unless detailed interviewing procedures were employed and this has rarely been the case. Findings of verbal conditioning without awareness for bright, relatively sophisticated college students have been reported much less frequently than when the same procedures are employed with patient populations (Spielberger *et al.,* 1962).

The importance of instructions. It seems reasonable to assume that many subjects, especially college students, approach psychological experiments with implicit problem-solving sets which lead them to develop hypotheses about what they are supposed to do. The interviews with subjects who participated in Experiments I-IV revealed that most of those who were not aware of correct or correlated contingencies had hypotheses about the experiment and the reinforcement. The fact that learning instructions in Experiment III produced more aware subjects suggests that when subjects are given explicitly a problem-solving set, they proceed more directly to test out their hypotheses about the experiment. Learning instructions also produced more subjects who had positive attitudes toward the reinforcement. If the subjects given learning instructions figured out what the experimenter wanted them to do, they tended to be more willing to comply because of their stronger desire to receive the reinforcement. Thus, instructions appear to affect both awareness and performance in verbal-conditioning experiments.

The nature of the verbal-conditioning task. Kanfer and McBrearty (1961) have pointed out that difficulties in stimulus discrimination may affect awareness and learning in verbal-conditioning experiments. When a conditioning procedure in which there is relatively little stimulus control, such as Greenspoon's (1955) word-naming task, is employed in contrast to procedures in which there is considerable stimulus control, such as the sentence-construction task employed in the experiments reported in this paper, fewer subjects are likely to become aware. Kanfer and McBrearty have demonstrated that on conditioning tasks in which the reinforced response class is more easily identified more subjects became aware. The findings of Matarazzo *et al.* (1960) have called attention to essentially the same phenomenon when the response class *humans* was reinforced as compared to when the response class *plurals* was reinforced.

It is not too surprising that when superficial interviews are employed with unstructured or highly abstract verbal-conditioning tasks, evidence for learning without awareness is more frequently reported. Under such conditions subjects would encounter greater difficulties in determining what was expected of them and would be more likely to develop correlated hypotheses. Subjects with correlated hypotheses tend to be judged unaware on the bases of their responses to brief postconditioning interviews. Dulany's (1961) work with Greenspoon's (1955) word-naming task clearly indicated that correlated hypotheses were more frequent when a less structured conditioning procedure was employed. With the relatively structured conditioning task employed in the four experiments reported here, most subjects were either aware of a correct response-reinforcement contingency or were unaware of such a contingency; only three subjects (all given neutral instructions) developed correlated hypotheses.

Eriksen (1960) has recently pointed out that "attention" rather than "awareness" may be the important variable in studies of learning without awareness, and that in situations where cues and reinforcements are salient enough to produce learning they will not escape detection by awareness. The experiments reported here would seem to offer support for Eriksen's conclusion. To be sure, the findings in our studies do not provide evidence that learning cannot take place without awareness, but merely affirm Adams' (1957) observation that such evidence has not been demonstrated convincingly in the laboratory.

Summary

The general goal of this paper was to examine the role of awareness in verbal conditioning. The concepts of learning and awareness as employed in investigations of verbal conditioning were analyzed and the results of four verbal-conditioning experiments were reported. In these studies, a sentence-construction task was employed as the conditioning procedure and "Good" was the reinforcing stimulus. Awareness was inferred on the basis of subjects' responses to a detailed postconditioning interview conducted immediately following conditioning trials.

The results of the four experiments were interpreted as supporting the hypothesis that "what is learned" in verbal-conditioning experiments is awareness of a response-reinforcement contingency. The extent to which subjects acted upon what they had learned seemed to depend upon how much they wanted to receive the reinforcement. Interpretation of the results of the four studies within the framework of cognitive-learning theory appeared to be most useful for generating specific hypotheses which led to observations in the data of previously unreported relationships between performance on the conditioning task and different aspects of the subjects' awareness. Experimental conditions which are likely to influence the results of verbal-conditioning experiments were discussed.

References

Adams, J. Laboratory studies of behavior without awareness. *Psychol. Bull.*, 1957, 54, 383-405.

Buss, A. H., & Gerjuoy, Irma R. Verbal conditioning and anxiety. *J. abnorm. soc. Psychol.*, 1958, 57, 249-250.

Buss, A. H., Gerjuoy, Irma R., & Zussman, J. Verbal conditioning and extinction with verbal and nonverbal reinforcers. *J. exp. Psychol.*, 1958, 56, 139-145.

Campbell, D. T. Operational delineation of "what is learned" via the transposition experiment. *Psychol. Rev.*, 1954, 61, 167-174.

Church, Jane C. The relationship between indices of awareness and performance in verbal conditioning. Unpublished honors thesis, Duke University, 1961.

Cohen, B. D., Kalish, H. I., Thurston, J. R., & Cohen, E. Experimental manipulation of verbal behavior. *J. exp. Psychol.*, 1954, 47, 106-110.

DiVesta, F., & Blake, Kathryn. The effects of instructional "sets" on learning and transfer. *Amer. J. Psychol.*, 1959, 72, 57-67.

Dollard, J., & Miller, N. E. *Personality and psychotherapy.* New York: McGraw-Hill, 1950.

Dulany, D. E. Review of *Verbal behavior* by B. F. Skinner. *Science*, 1959, 129, 143-144.

Dulany, D. E. Hypotheses and habits in verbal "operant conditioning." *J. abnorm. soc. Psychol.*, 1961, 63, 251-263.

Eriksen, C. W. Unconscious processes. In M. R. Jones (Ed.), *Nebraska symposium on motivation.* Lincoln: Univer. Nebraska Press, 1958. Pp. 169-227.

Eriksen, C. W. Discrimination and learning without awareness. *Psychol. Rev.*, 1960, 67, 279-300.

Garner, W. R., Hake, H. W., & Eriksen, C. W. Operationism and the concept of perception. *Psychol. Rev.*, 1956, 63, 149-159.

Greenspoon, J. The reinforcing effect of two spoken sounds on the frequency of two responses. *Amer. J. Psychol.*, 1955, 68, 409-416.

Kanfer, F. H., & McBrearty, J. F. Verbal conditioning: Discrimination and awareness. *J. Psychol.*, 1961, 52, 115-124.

Kendler, H. H. "What is learned?"—A theoretical blind alley. *Psychol. Rev.*, 1952, 59, 269-277.

Kimble, G. A. *Hilgard & Marquis' Conditioning and learning.* (2nd ed.) New York: Appleton-Century-Crofts, Inc., 1961.

Krasner, L. Studies of the conditioning of verbal behavior. *Psychol. Bull.*, 1958, 55, 148-170.

Krasner, L., Weiss, R. L., & Ullman, L. P.   Responsivity to verbal conditioning as a function of two different measures of "awareness."   *Amer.
Psychologist,* 1959, 14, 388.

Krieckhaus, E. E., & Eriksen, C. W.   A study of awareness and its effect on
learning and generalization.   *J. Pers.,* 1960, 28, 503-517.

Leventhal, A. M.   The effects of diagnostic category and reinforcer on
learning without awareness.   *J. abnorm. soc. Psychol.,* 1959, 59, 162-
166.

Levin, S. M.   The effects of awareness on verbal conditioning.   *J. exp.
Psychol.,* 1961, 61, 67-75.

Mandler, G., & Kaplan, W. K.   Subjective evaluation and reinforcing effect
of a verbal stimulus.   *Science,* 1956, 124, 582-583.

Matarazzo, J. D., Saslow, G., & Pareis, E. N.   Verbal conditioning of two
response classes: Some methodological considerations.   *J. abnorm. soc.
Psychol.,* 1960, 61, 190-206.

Salzinger, K.   Experimental manipulation of verbal behavior: A review.
J. gen. Psychol., 1959, 61, 65-94.

Skinner, B. F.   *Verbal behavior.*   New York: Appleton-Century-Crofts,
Inc., 1957.

Spielberger, C. D., Levin, S. M., & Shepard, Mary.   The effects of awareness
and attitude toward the reinforcement on the operant conditioning of
verbal behavior.   *J. Pers.,* 1962, 30, 106-121.

Taffel, C.   Anxiety and the conditioning of verbal behavior.   *J. abnorm.
soc. Psychol.,* 1955, 51, 496-501.

Tatz, S. J.   Symbolic activity in "learning without awareness."   *Amer. J.
Psychol.,* 1960, 73, 239-247.

Zener, K.   The significance of experience of the individual for the science
of psychology.   In Feigl, H., Scriven, M., & Maxwell, G., *Minnesota
studies in the philosophy of science,* Vol. 2.   Minneapolis: Univer.
Minn. Press, 1958.   Pp. 254-369.

The place of hypotheses and intentions: an analysis of verbal control in verbal conditioning[1]

Don E. Dulany, Jr., *University of Illinois*

It began innocently enough. But the literature of verbal operant conditioning (Krasner, 1958; Salzinger, 1959; Adams, 1957) has raised some uncommonly weighty problems—the experimental and theoretical status of awareness, the status of the subject's private reports in a learning or conditioning experiment, the question of conscious, voluntary as against automatic, involuntary control, and the generality of principles and procedures from the prelinguistic to the human level. These problems are raised mainly because the case for operant conditioning without awareness is so contestable. And that, ironically, comes in part from a rather strained fidelity to operant conditioning procedures.

Conditioning is often claimed for significant shifts from an operant level in the absence of controls, although we can a little less confidently rule out other time-correlated controls for speaking than for pecking. And questioning typically must await an extinction procedure, a procedure excellently suited to the disconfirmation of any hypotheses the subject may have had. Nor, for that matter, do we know what extinction should mean for this kind of acquisition. Should we think of verbal conditioning as a momentary change in response rate associated with a contingent stimulus, or as a fairly enduring change in availability of response? As it is, if rate of response declines during extinction, this may be taken as further evidence that conditioning has occurred. If it doesn't, this of course just shows how strong the conditioning was. Furthermore, as Adams (1957), Krasner (1958), and Eriksen (1960) have observed, the questions asked often

[1] The research described in this paper was supported by grants from the National Science Foundation, G-4461, and the National Institute of Mental Health, US PH M-3002.

seem inadequate and criteria of awareness vague and arbitrary. Nor can we usually rule out the possibility that correlated hypotheses may have mediated the effects, as Adams (1957) significantly notes. What may be more important in the long run, awareness as a concept has been given little of the theoretical relevance that would permit research to bear more directly on the more interesting questions the literature raises. Furthermore, a turn through thesis microfilms and a little hearsay scholarship will show an appreciable second literature, distinguished in the main by better control, negative results, and lack of publication. Only recently have a few critical studies begun to appear (Tatz, 1960; Matarazzo, Saslow, & Pareis, 1960; Azrin, Holz, Ulrich, & Goldiamond, 1961; Levin, 1961; Dulany, 1961; Spielberger, Levin, & Shepard, 1962).

In the present paper, I shall mention some of our earlier experiments, outline a theoretical network they suggest, and say more of some later experiments that explore that network. This is too much to talk about at once. It is my predicament, however, that I can give little meaning to the experiments without the methodology and theory, and little excuse for either without the experiments. The great interdependence of method, theory, and experiment in the investigation of verbal control calls for a joint presentation, if only in outline.

A few years ago my associates and I set about to obtain a stable finding of verbal conditioning without awareness so that we could investigate its parameters (Komosa, 1958; Floden, 1959; Tuite, 1960; Blaufarb, 1960; Dulany, 1960). We have yet to find it. Using all the common tasks, we compared experimentals with controls, questioning carefully after acquisition, and setting report of a correct or correlated hypothesis as the criterion of awareness— a choice that was not arbitrary, for reasons I shall give. All of it could seem most remarkable for our disinclination to accept the null hypothesis and turn to other matters. But in every study, subjects who reported a correct or possibly correlated hypothesis made themselves conspicuous with dramatic "conditioning" curves. It was, of course, the subjects' reports that had become the lure, reports that we had no mandate to believe, but which could not sensibly be dismissed when so clearly related to other behavior.

In our first attempt to analyze the subject's verbal control

(Dulany, 1961), we followed Greenspoon's (1955) procedure—
words ad libitum and a warm "Umhmm" for plural nouns. We
wanted first to see whether the subjects' reports of a behavioral
hypothesis would be related to selection of plural nouns. When
questioned, most subjects ventured only that they were supposed
to run through their associations so that we might study them. But
roughly a fourth reported that they were supposed to associate in
series, in the same category, whenever the experimenter said
"Umhmm" and to find a new category when he remained silent.
The others reported nothing as correct. As you can see (Fig. 1),
only the "reinforcement for association," or RFA, group "conditioned"—though strikingly.[2]

This is the mystery, and a challenge for theory. But from
those reports let us infer a semantic associative set after plural
nouns as stimuli and a nonassociative set after other words. We
have no reason to infer that alignment of sets for controls because
they give no report of the critical hypothesis. We do have a
difference in plural selection between controls and RFA subjects
to account for. We might therefore hypothesize that plural response to a prior plural is related to an associative as opposed to
a nonassociative set. This could well be, if the subject's organization of verbal habits is such that when he gives a semantic associate
he tends also to give a grammatical associate. "Diamonds," when
one continues a series, should bring "rubies" or "pearls"—plurals.

To examine this *post hoc* hypothesis we *instructed* subjects to
do what they had *reported* they were supposed to do. From the
protocols of Experiment I 100 plural nouns and 100 other words
were taken at random and used as stimuli in a word-association
procedure. For half the words the subject responded under an·
associative set and for half under a nonassociative set. Casting
each subject's response to plurals into a contingency table, we
found plural noun vs. other response to be significantly related to
an associative vs. a nonassociative set, for 17 straight subjects.
In this reinforcement contingency, "I am supposed to associate in
a series when you say 'Umhmm' " looks very like a correlated hypothesis for "I am supposed to say plural nouns."

[2] All trend tests reported as significant yielded F's with p values less than .01,
and in most cases higher levels of significance were attained. When described as
nonsignificant, F's did not reach the .05 level.

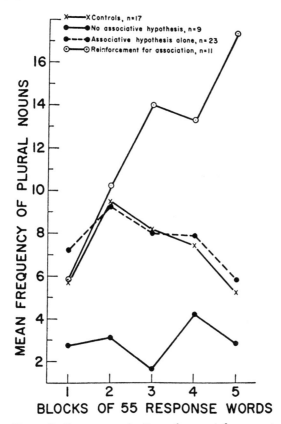

Figure 1. Response selection of nonreinforcement controls and subjects reporting three types of behavioral hypothesis.

What was done in these two experiments may seem very reasonable to many—and perhaps not to others. If it does seem reasonable, I think it is because instruction, report, and response selection enter into a web of hypotheses that are so much a part of our thinking that they were comfortably assumed. Probably the least comfortable is the assumption that a subject when questioned does report a prior behavioral hypothesis, but that assumption seems somehow supported by what was done with the instructions of the second experiment. Nearly everyone thinks that instruction will produce some kind of awareness, or behavioral hypothesis, and a set to respond accordingly. Our inference to sets from the subjects' reports must certainly cross an assumption that the be-

havioral hypothesis he reports is associated with some self-instructional set. And shouldn't an instructional set—self or social—
result in a response? Perhaps it makes some sense to expect reports and instructions to have a similar relation to behavior because they enter into a common set of familiar hypotheses—hypotheses that guided what we did and seem supported by it. All
of this is simply to emphasize that if we try to analyze the subjects'
verbal control through the use of reports and instructions—and
I cannot as yet think of any better way to go about it—we are
caught in a net of theory. I think we would do well to make that
theoretical network explicit enough to be useful.

A theoretical network

I shall present nothing that could be represented as a finished
and closed theory. A theoretical network is by its nature open.
This is merely a set of interconnecting theoretical propositions,
none of which are new, and most of which are too old and common
even to attribute proper credit. They come to me in this particular
arrangement mainly out of our own experiments. Certain features
are similar to recent emphases of Luria (1960), Zaporozhets
(1958), and Miller, Galanter, and Pribram (1960), to mention
only a few. But to compare and contrast these positions would
take another kind of paper.

In the upper left of Figure 2 you can see reinforcement hypotheses (RH) and their hypothesized antecedents. There are
several things subjects may hypothesize about a consequence and
could be told about it: A, that it signifies that a preceding response
is correct; B, that it merely follows a certain response—when that
response happens to be scored correct; C, only that it occurred; or,
D, that none occurred. So let us hypothesize that reinforcement
instructions A through D may induce these reinforcement hypotheses A through D. We shall think of RH A through D as a
variable and see if it is a useful one. Of course, any of these
hypotheses might emerge as a result of other, noninstructional
manipulations. As a first anchor among them, let us reasonably
hypothesize that RH A through D will be associated with the
treatments selective, random, and no reinforcement.

If we should instruct the subject that some response class is
correct, he should entertain a corresponding behavioral hypothesis.

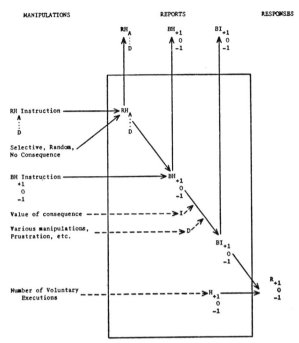

Figure 2. A theoretical network stating hypothetical relations among certain manipulations, reinforcement hypotheses (RH); behavioral hypotheses (BH); behavioral intentions(BI); habit (H); subjective incentive value (I); drive (D); RH, BH, and BI reports; and response selection.

And that hypothesis should tend to be associated, though usually imperfectly, with a corresponding self-instructional set, or as we might as well call it, behavioral intention. We have only begun to examine determinants of the degree of that association—hence the dotted lines—but we have some evidence that certain motivational variables and the incentive value of the consequence (Oltman, 1960) have important roles. In the usual verbal-conditioning experiment, where those variables are unmanipulated, they should vary randomly over subjects, and the BH-BI relation should be positive but imperfect. And a behavioral intention, once formed, should tend to persist and select members of the corresponding response class.

Once having questioned our subjects and looked at their behavior, their reports must take a prominent place in the network.

Simply put, we hypothesize that a subject, questioned in a way to be described, should tend to report his reinforcement and behavioral hypotheses, and also his behavioral intentions.

But, as we have found, subjects report not only a correct response class as correct, but any of various response classes. And the experimenter may instruct the use of any response class he can name, not just the one he happens to score correct. What we require is a principle by which to array those possibilities on a single, useful variable. We have already seen (Dulany, 1961) a likely choice—orders of correlation of an instructed or reported response class with a correct response class. Now, obviously, presence and absence of members of any response class will show some order of correlation—including zero—with presence and absence of members of a correct response class. This is banal but useful. A subject instructed to speak of his early experiences tends to use first person pronouns. Instructed to speak of others he tends not to. And instructed to pick the first word that strikes his eye, he might do neither. Whatever the origin of these response correlations—and it should often be in the subject's prior organization of habits—they appear in this network as parameters that must always be considered. Sometimes we can determine the order of correlation directly. At other times, as we shall see, it will be useful to hypothesize it and evaluate that hypothesis along with others.

Thus we arrive at arrays of response classes, behavioral intentions, and so through the network. Put more precisely, and as can be seen in Figure 2, the central hypotheses of the network state associations among those arrays.

The term "verbal control" is used here and there, rarely precisely, but usually with a meaning not far from that here. I shall use the term to summarize the set of theoretical propositions relating response selection to hypotheses and intentions—whether they be verbal, partially verbal, or entirely cognitive-neural, so long as they are verbalizable. And it should not offend ancient usage to call the relation of a behavioral intention to its response class "voluntary control."

The lower part of the network has not been the focus of our attention so far but must be considered. A theory that holds intention to precede all response explains too much, and, in an old-fashioned sense, is certainly false. I cannot here go into the various possible bases for distinguishing voluntary and involuntary control—Peak (1933), Gibson (1941), Skinner (1938), Hilgard and Marquis (1940), and Kimble (1961), among many, have—but the problem cannot be avoided once the human subject in a learning or conditioning experiment is directly instructed or allowed to report. I must at least provide here for the response that *can* occur on instruction or self-instruction when it occurs with neither. In our experiments, some response classes (first person pronouns, hostile verbs) show time-correlated increases in frequency unassociated with either reports, instruction, or reinforcement. It is as though situational cues release the response in transfer—involuntarily. So we may say that a habit is manifest when such a response occurs in correlation with cues, and unassociated with any correlated instruction or correlated reports. This is one kind of "involuntary control"—perhaps the kind manifest in many highly routine activities. For a necessary anchor, one that we are now investigating, I take an old hypothesis seriously revived by Miller *et al.* (1960), and mentioned incidentally by too many to name: this kind of habit should be some function of the number of voluntary executions of the response in association with cues. Whether or not the more common reinforcements will produce it is controversial (Adams, 1957; Eriksen, 1960; Postman & Sassenrath, 1961). In view of strong criticism of studies with positive findings, and the repeated negative findings of our own and others, I think there is value in entertaining and examining a highly plausible alternative.

This is rather an extravagance of theory in order to say that a human subject does what he thinks he is supposed to do if he wants to, unless, of course, it's all a matter of habit—pure and simple. But the theory does say a little more than that, and in a way that suggests at least the following four uses.

1. If we can position both the subject's reports and "what is reported" within a theoretical network, the reports become more theoretically relevant and experimentally useful. Report validity takes the status of a hypothesis, and we become concerned to see whether the reports behave as the theory holds they should. And if they do, that hypothesis, like any other, is inductively supported. To rely upon a phenomenological observation language would require a more confident acceptance of those reports than is war-

ranted, perhaps, when there is good reason to think (Eriksen, 1960) that they have only imperfect, probabilistic validity. Most would agree that a hypothesis may be considered empirically meaningful if it implies observationally supportable consequences (Carnap, 1956; Feigl, 1956). We would be compelled to recognize that some hypotheses may have to be conjoined with others in order to have those deductive consequences (Hempel, 1952; Carnap, 1956). The trouble with a hypothesis concerning the validity of a report on a private event—like most hypotheses mentioning an unobservable—is that it is too weak in isolation to be productive. Thus one value of a theoretical network is that the hypothesis of report validity can be interconnected with others in such a way that they may jointly imply experimental consequences. In short, a meaningful hypothesis of report validity presupposes a theory—a theory that will have consequences allowing for the inductive support of that hypothesis. Of course, as for any hypothetical relation, we must specify its conditions: relatively simple response classes, our general experimental situations, and some such system of questioning and categorization as I shall describe.

This discussion draws on the same logic of science as has discussion of the construct validity of tests (Cronbach & Meehl, 1955). It provides an alternative to try—an alternative to a phenomenological data language, dismissal of the subject's reports, or the collection of interesting correlations of response selection with reports that we are forbidden to interpret.

2. The theoretical network specifies the evolving meaning of "hypotheses" and "intentions," terms that, given our problem, would be less satisfactorily related to observables by operational definition than through hypotheses. As originally proposed (Bridgman, 1927), and as precisely formulated (Bergman, 1951), operational definitions are explicit definitions—single, complete, stipulative. They specify the condition for the use of a term, a test presentation-test result, not, be it re-emphasized, the relation of an operation to a hypothetical process, state, or entity. But this is little help when we suspect that certain verbally articulated or cognitive-neural processes may result from various manipulations and then participate in the selection of responses. A verbally articulated hypothesis or intention is a sequence of motor re-

sponses, and when unobserved, a hypothetical process or state, not just a term we conveniently associate with an experimental operation. Furthermore, on intuition and/or unwillingness in each case to accept the alternative, I shall assume (a) that I am at this moment aware—experiencing, conscious; (b) that my experimental subjects do not differ from me in this general capability; (c) that this awareness is neurally mediated; and (d) that aspects of this awareness behave as variables lawfully related among themselves and to experimental variables. I conclude that our problem requires a concern for certain hypothetical processes or states and their relation to each other and to observables. But to venture the relation of an hypothetical process or state to an observable—and of course of one unobservable to another—requires an hypothesis, not a classical operational definition.

There is, of course, a very common and looser use—or misuse —of the term "operational definition" in conjunction with the general assumption of hypothetical process variables. The awkward implications of this usage would be well illustrated by speaking of "hypotheses" and "intentions" as operationally defined by instructions or reports. In the first place, these are terms in use— in use in much informal and vernacular theory that may crudely approximate the relations of certain hypothetical processes to each other and to observables. The present network merely selects, organizes, and very slightly refines some of that informal and vernacular theory. We cannot operationally define these terms in any way we please and still expect to investigate the problems they suggest or the hypotheses they carry. To defend the appropriateness of the operation to the construct we should have to show that it is related to other variables as we would expect the construct to be, thereby at the same time empirically evaluating the defining statement. And we must specify the conditions in which we expect a report or an instruction to be related, only probabilistically, to one of these constructs, as we would for an hypothesis, not a definition. If a defining statement is not arbitrary, if it is to be qualified and somehow evaluated by the evidence, I think that we can more straightforwardly call it an hypothesis.

The nature of our problem has led us to draw upon recent clarifications in the logic of science (Hempel, 1952; Carnap, 1956; Feigl, 1956), and to introduce these theoretical terms by tentatively positioning them within a theoretical network. "Reinforcement hypothesis," "behavioral hypothesis," and "behavioral intention" are given whatever meaning they have here by the set of supportable hypotheses they enter into. Their "place" is in a theoretical network. And their meaning rides with the hypotheses, to be supported or augmented or revised, as they must, in response to the data. Because the hypotheses connect those terms with experimental variables, that meaning is empirical. Because any theoretical sentence is tentative, and new ones may always be added, the network, and therefore the constructs, are open. For example, those constructs will be further enriched if we can add and support theoretical sentences relating reinforcement hypotheses and behavioral hypotheses to figurality of the consequence and correct response class, to problem-solving instructions, and to other informational variables.

Some (Campbell & Fiske, 1959; Bechtoldt, 1959) have noted the similarity of the use of a theoretical network to the use of converging operations (Garner, Hake, & Eriksen, 1956), which are said to give partial, multiple, operational definition of hypothetical processes. But on the authors' explication of the term "converging," the operations are seen to be experimental observations, at least one inductively supporting hypotheses in which the theoretical construct term appears, and at least one tending to disconfirm an alternative theoretical interpretation of the first observation. Thus the logic of converging operations seems in substance covered by the broader logic of theoretical networks. For reasons given, however, the language of theory rather than of operational definition seems a better clarification of what we are in this case doing; and the fuller use of a theoretical network has certain other advantages discussed in the preceding and following points.

3. The network provides a conception of awareness—namely, a correct or correlated hypothesis—that is related to response selection by common theoretical propositions. "Awareness" does not enter into either the language of operant conditioning or a theory of automatic strengthening, the two formulations that have dominated research in this area. In the verbal-conditioning literature, awareness has usually been an embarrassment to be ignored, or an artifact to be designed out of better experiments, apparently

so that more fundamental lawful relations might be revealed. But with careful duplicity of the experimenter and an extended series of trials, investigators produce, at best, small and highly questionable shifts in response without awareness. With instruction or reports of awareness, subjects shift remarkably. Awareness should enter into lawful relationships no less fundamental than any other, and we may have been throwing away the best part. With an awareness encompassed by theory, an alternative strategy of research becomes more appealing. As a dividend, this is also a conception of awareness relevant to another theoretical concern. A classical theory of automatic strengthening clearly implies that learning should occur in the absence of a correct or correlated behavioral hypothesis.

4. The final use, of course, is the more conventional one of suggesting experiments that may support the present formulation in competition with others.

Experimental evidence

We turned again to the most widely used verbal-conditioning task, one devised by Taffel (1955). Subjects took one of several pronouns from a card and formed a sentence, while we reinforced I or We with "Good," after a first block of 20 trials. After 80 trials we asked what has, with minor variations, become a standard set of questions (Table 1). Questions 1 to 3 are directed to the subject's reinforcement hypothesis, question 4 goes to his behavioral hypothesis, and question 5 to his behavioral intention. As a result of much trial and error, we have arrived at a set of questions

Table 1. Post experimental questions.

---

1. a. Did you notice whether or not I said anything during the experiment? b. (What?)
2. a. Did you come to think it was random or did it follow anything in particular that you did?
   b. (What?)
3. a. Did you come to think there was or wasn't any purpose or significance to the "Good" in this experiment? b. (What?)
4. a. Did you come to think that there was anything you were supposed to say, or not say, on each trial in order to be correct—something the experimenter wanted you to say or not say? b. (What?) c. (Did you come to think there was or wasn't any kind of correct response?)
5. a. How did you go about making up your sentences? b. How did you go about selecting a word from the bottom of the card? c. (Would you say that you did or didn't try to use any particular words or kinds of sentences?) d. (What?)

---

intended to go as directly as possible to the relevant dimension without suggesting to the subject where on that dimension he should place himself. Vague and ambiguous questions, we find, frequently produce vague and ambiguous answers.

The reports must, of course, be categorized (see Table 2). Categories for reinforcement hypotheses match those of the network. But for reports of hypotheses and intentions we are obliged to break up the theoretical dimension running from perfect positive to perfect negative correlation. The principle is this: The categories must bracket ranges of the dimension we can recognize— which is to say, orders of correlation we can reliably hypothesize.

Table 2. Categories of reports.

Report of Behavioral Hypotheses: The subject. . .

    I. names the correct response class and calls it correct or describes it as what he is supposed to do or as what E wants him to do.

    II. names as correct (or as what he is supposed to do or what E wants him to do) some response class that is positively, but imperfectly, correlated with the correct response class.

    III. does not name the correct response class as correct. He may report that he does not know the correct response, that he does not know whether there is a correct response, that there is not a correct response, or he may report some uncorrelated and irrelevant response class as correct. (An irrelevant response class is one that is uncorrelated but not incompatible with the correct response class.)

    IV. names as correct some response class that is uncorrelated but partially incompatible with the correct response class—e.g., right-left alternation or position preference when the correct response is randomly distributed right and left.

    V. names as correct some incorrect response class that is negatively correlated with the correct response class.

Report of Reinforcement Hypotheses: The subject. . .

    A. reports the *significance* of the contingent stimulus—that it signified that the preceding response was correct or what E wanted or would agree with. It is described as having some selective reinforcement or informative value, not as a general encouragement to continue.

    B. reports the *distribution* but not the significance of the contingent stimulus—that it followed the response class E designates as correct.

    C. reports the *occurrence* but neither the significance nor the distribution of the contingent stimulus.

    D. does *not* report occurrence of the contingent stimulus.

Report of Behavioral Intentions: The subject. . .

    1. reports intention to produce the response class E designates as correct.

    2. reports intention to produce some response class that is positively, but imperfectly, correlated with the correct response class.

    3. reports no particular intention or reports intention to produce some irrelevant response class.

    4. reports intention to produce some response class that is uncorrelated but partially incompatible with the correct response class.

    5. reports intention to produce some response class that is negatively correlated with the correct response class.

Category I is the correct hypothesis—a perfectly correlated hypothesis. Category II is a positive but imperfectly correlated hypothesis—for instance, "sentences about my childhood." Category III catches the report of no response class, or of some uncorrelated and irrelevant response class. Category IV also brackets uncorrelated hypotheses, but these name some response class that is also partially incompatible with the correct response class—for example, "the word on the right." These latter two categories should be distinguished wherever there is prior reason, as we have had, to expect some time-correlated increase in the correct response class. When this is the case, the base for no verbal control is a slight increase and verbal control of type IV should tend to wash it out. Category V covers reports of a negatively correlated hypothesis—for example, "talking about other people."

The categories of report for behavioral intention parallel those for behavioral hypothesis. For any response class we wonder not only whether it is reported as correct, but also whether it is reported as intended. And we say that a subject reports an intention of using a response class when he says it was something he was trying to do, or something deliberate or intentional. The question is not so simple as "Are the subjects really reporting a behavioral intention when they say these things?" For now, we think a behavioral intention is, *among other things,* something that should be reported in this way. The question is whether subjects say these things in proper relation to the other variables that also help to specify a behavioral intention.

To a degree they apparently do. Questions and categories could certainly be improved, but the reports were sorted with acceptable reliability—that is, two persons tended to hypothesize the same orders of response-class correlations. We see, too, that the procedure yields a useful variable from which to predict response selection. Now, if the subjects report correctly, if behavioral intentions do produce response selection, and if the response correlations were correctly estimated, we should expect ordered differences in performance among the several levels of BI report. The difference among group slopes, shown in Figure 3, is highly significant.

Add to these hypotheses the hypothesis of a BH-BI relation, and we should also expect levels of report of behavioral hypotheses to

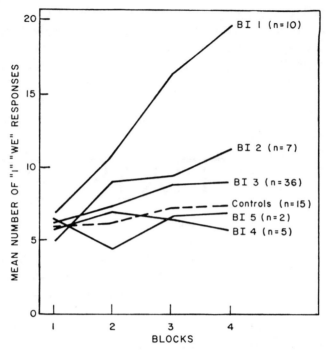

Figure 3. Response selection of nonreinforcement controls and of experimental subjects at each of five levels of report of behavioral intentions, with selective reinforcement of "I" and "We" with "Good."

be related to response selection. And in a comparable analysis they were. We cannot, however, strongly expect levels of report of reinforcement hypotheses to be significantly related to response selection, if we are, in fact, adding links to a chain of imperfectly associated variables; and they were not. But if we are, then the correlations of levels of the three kinds of report with a response shift or behavioral change measure should fall off in the order BI, BH, RH. The correlations are, in fact, .71, .57, .36—each significantly less than the preceding.

But there is a better way to put the question. What we must predict is that only levels of report of behavioral intentions will show an intrinsic relation to behavioral change with the other two report variables partialled out. In fact, we find that the second-order partial for BI reports and behavioral change (BC) is .57. For BH reports and BC it is .23, and for RH reports and BC .06, neither significant. This is what we should expect if reinforcement hypotheses and behavioral hypotheses affect performance only through behavioral intentions and not directly. The evidence should not permit theory to leave the human performer buried in his hypotheses.

We should also predict very definite relations among the report variables themselves. If reinforcement hypotheses influence behavioral intentions only through the mediation of behavioral hypotheses, then the first-order partial for RH and BI reports should not be significant. It is .09. But, of course, the other two first-order partials should be appreciable: they are .46 for RH and BH and .48 for BH and BI.

It remains only to ask whether there are any effects that do not follow from the hypotheses of verbal control—any response selection without awareness or intention. Comparing the BH-III's and then the BI-3's with controls in trend analyses, we found no evidence of either. Since Postman and Sassenrath (1961) have emphasized that automatic strengthening should occur for subjects who perceive the reinforcement as confirming, we also compared those subjects—the III-A-3's in this system—with controls, but again there was no significant effect. But in all three of those analyses we did find time-correlated increases in I and We —without reports of intention or awareness—increases that would seem to be the manifestations of prior habit.

Certainly this could seem an eccentric methodology—especially this use of correlational analysis—and part of its justification will have to come from consistency in systematic replications. With the assumption of direction of causality, only the additional assumption of linearity of regression need be made, and this is not too seriously violated. But we can, if we wish, regard these r's as only descriptive of the relations among the numbers we have and forego statistical inference for replication. In one systematic replication the task was similar but a class of amusement words was reinforced (Figure 4). In another we reinforced Binder's (1957) class of hostile verbs (Figure 5). The second-order partials for each report variable and behavioral change have a reassuring consistency, as shown by Table 3. And much the same can be said for relations among the report variables (Table 4).

But what of instruction? From this theoretical network we should expect the same kind of relationship between experimental

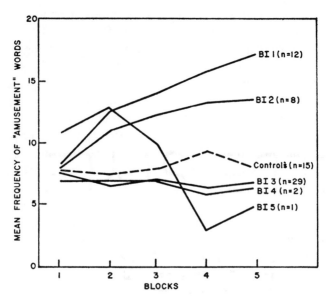

Figure 4. Response selection of nonreinforcement controls and of experimental subjects at each of five levels of report of behavioral intentions, with selective reinforcement of amusement words with "Good."

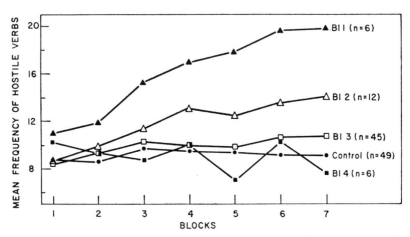

Figure 5. Response selection of nonreinforcement controls and of experimental subjects at each of four levels of report of behavioral intentions, with selective reinforcement of hostile verbs by "Good."

Table 3. Second-Order partial *r*'s relating each of three report variables to behavioral change in three separate experiments.

	I, We N = 60	Amusement Words N = 52	Hostile Verbs N = 67
BC, BI·BH, RH...........	.57	.77	.65
BC, BH·BI, RH...........	.23*	.14	.003
BC, RH·BH, BI...........	.06	.02	−.15

* p about .09.

Table 4. First-Order partial *r*'s among three report variables in three separate experiments.

	I, We N = 60	Amusement Words N = 52	Hostile Verbs N = 67
BI, BH·RH...............	.48	.48	.66
BH, RH·BI...............	.46	.40	.44
BI, RH·BH...............	.09	.003	−.13

performance and the five levels of behavioral instruction that we find for the corresponding five levels of report. And if this should be the case, this would be further evidence that the reports have behaved as they should. Of course, with instructions uniformly administered after the first block of trials, the effects should be even clearer. For a more vivid picture of the relative contributions of a behavioral instruction and a consequence, we varied them factorially—our five levels of instruction and two of consequence, "Good" and nothing. With clear effects expected, 40 subjects seemed enough for the design. From Figures 6 and 7 there can be little doubt that instruction is an impressive control, with or without the reinforcement that did not produce a significant effect.

I must also briefly describe a further experiment in this series because reinforcement hypotheses—as well as behavioral hypotheses—were manipulated with instructions. This time we reinforced a diffuse class of 100 active words, all of which had mean ratings at the extreme of an active–inactive scale from Osgood's semantic differential. In one condition subjects were informed, after a first block of 20 trials, both of the correct response class, "active words," and of the role of the consequence—that it signified that the preceding response was correct. In a second condition,

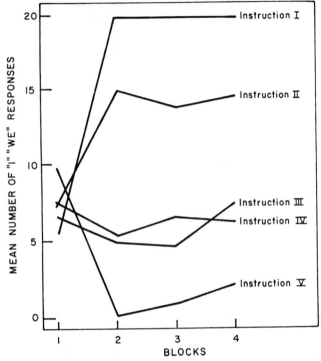

Figure 6. Response selection of subjects at each of five levels
of behavioral instruction; selective reinforcement of "I" and
"We" with "Good."

subjects were informed only of the correct response class, and in a
third condition, only of the role of the consequence. In a
fourth condition no behavioral or reinforcement instructions were
given. Three levels of consequence—avoidance of an electric
shock, "Umhmm," and a tone—complete a 4 × 3 design with
repeated measures. Of course, in this circumstance, the network
allows for the emergence of further hypotheses as a consequence
of other manipulations, but we were interested in the effect of hypotheses manipulated by instructions. We therefore questioned as
usual and retained for this analysis only those subjects reporting
at their instructed level, with 10 subjects per cell, a total of 120.
Figure 8 clearly displays some kind of response selection, but it is
not significantly related to the three levels of consequence. Figure
9 shows the difference among levels of instructed hypotheses, and
this effect is of course highly significant.

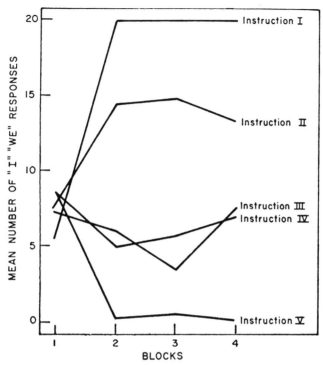

Figure 7. Response selection of subjects at each of five levels of behavioral instruction; no reinforcement.

But is it just being aware of the correct response class that has an effect or is there also a direct effect of an instructed reinforcement hypothesis? Disregarding the insignificant classification for consequence, we can rearrange these data in a further, 2 × 2 design—informed of the correct response class vs. not and informed of the role of the reinforcement vs. not. This provides the opportunity to confirm with instruction what we have found for report. Consistently enough, the effect for instructed BH is significant but not for instructed RH. And I should add that none of the groups uninformed of the correct response class differed in slope from an additional 20 controls. Thus there was no evidence of response selection through reinforcement and semantic mediation alone, with or without awareness of the role of reinforcement. Response selection came only with awareness of the correct response class.

Finally, the network as outlined allows us to formulate a rather difficult question in a researchable way. Given some variable that

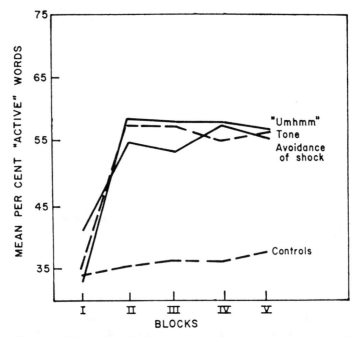

Figure 8. Response selection of nonreinforcement controls and of experimental subjects with each of three consequences of selection of an active word (40 subjects per group; 20 controls).

might be related to a verbal-conditioning measure, what will its locus of effect be? Will it be voluntary or involuntary? Many studies have reported the relation of conditioning without awareness to a number of personal and interpersonal variables (e.g., Sarason, 1958; Sapolsky, 1960). But with reason to question the assessment of awareness, these variables could well have operated on the subjects' voluntary control—that is, on the degree of association of behavioral hypotheses with behavioral intentions. Nor do the results of these experiments show that any possible involuntary effects are differential-acquisition rather than differential-transfer effects. To do that, the design must keep the personal or interpersonal variable orthogonal to the consequence.

We asked the question for one such variable, an experimental frustration that we hypothesized would produce hostility. Consider again the experiment in which we reinforced selection of a hostile verb with "Good." We ran 40 controls and enough experimental subjects to have 40 reporting at BH-III and BI-3—no

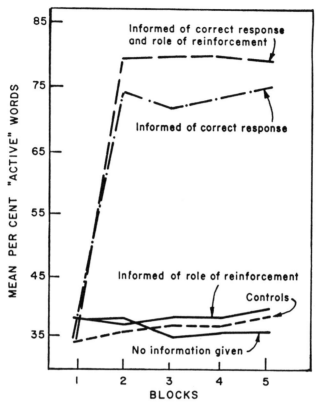

Figure 9. Response selection of nonreinforcement controls and experimental subjects at each of four combinations of behavioral and reinforcement instruction (30 subjects per group; 20 controls).

relevant behavioral hypotheses or intentions. Frustrating 20 in each group gave a 2×2 design. To arouse hostility after a first block of 20 trials, the experimenter asked a few difficult questions, and a few others that any literate person should be able to answer. The subjects' errors were then treated with considerable derision. (Dean Rusk, we learned, is head of the ag school; Franco, the communist dictator of France; and Verdi? That must be some kind of color.) Now if there are any general drive or drive-cue effects on acquisition without awareness—and we have provided for both possibilities—there should be an interaction of frustration and consequence. The difference in slope between experimentals and controls should be greater for hostile than for nonhostile subjects. The interaction was not significant; nor was there a significant main

effect for consequence that would show acquisition without awareness. Still, if there is an involuntary, differential transfer effect,
the frustration–nonfrustration effect should be significant. It was
not, though a significant over-all slope suggests that hostile verbs
can transfer without awareness in response to time-correlated cues.
But if the frustration had any effect it was apparently through the
subjects' voluntary control, through his reported intention to use
the response class he reported correct. Looking at all 67 experimental subjects covering the range of BH and BI reports, we see
that the BH-BI relation is .85 for frustrated subjects and .52 for
the nonfrustrated subjects—a difference that is significant ($p <$
.005), though not yet replicated.

I think that this question of locus of effects—whether they are
verbal and voluntary or habitual and involuntary—is fundamental
and can be sensibly asked. My guess that the answer may very
well be different for different variables is part of a general guess
that voluntary control and involuntary control participate in partially different sets of lawful relationships.

Operant conditioning, automatic strengthening, and verbal control

Can we still call the response selection we find operant conditioning? Passing over a few differences in procedure, perhaps
we can, though the question seems less important now. Response
classes repeatedly come under the functional control of a contingent
stimulus, at least for some subjects. But the language of operant
conditioning, as it has been extended to the verbal-conditioning
experiment, apparently gives no description of the differences in
performance that accompany the reports we get. Even when reinforcing a verbal response, operant conditioning might better be
kept a mute encounter if it would avoid what its language does
not describe. Nor does it seem strategically wise to have set a lack
of awareness as a programmatic condition for the demonstration of
verbal operant conditioning (see Verplanck, 1955, pp. 597-601).
Whether there is an account of all this within Skinner's (1953;
1957) extended system is another matter.

Are there other theoretical interpretations of these findings?
In principle there must be, perhaps more elegant ones, and doubt-
less some of these interpretations could be translated into another
theoretical language. Putting aside the effects of instruction for

the moment, the immediate data only show relations of reports among themselves and to response selection, not that anything reported participated in response selection. The hypotheses of report validity and verbal control—as well as of automatic strengthening—are of course only indirectly rather than directly supportable. But any interpretation that this is still learning by some process of automatic strengthening must supply other assumptions to account for the distinct pattern of relations of several kinds of reports among themselves and to learning—a pattern that follows fairly naturally from a theory of verbal control. One naturally thinks that the questions might have suggested the reports. Or subjects might feel obliged to rationalize their behavior. Or perhaps the hypotheses and intentions could even be some kind of phenomenal or linguistic emergent of the process of automatic strengthening itself. Or, for all we know, enough reinforcement to produce automatic strengthening is enough to arouse and select verbal hypotheses and intentions.

But whatever their face plausibility, these possibilities would entail further assumptions and a few unresolved questions. On what assumption, for instance, should behavioral intentions be more emergent than behavioral hypotheses? Consistently we find that BI reports are more strongly related to response selection than are BH reports. Or why do reinforcement hypotheses, if they are suggested, happen to be associated with behavioral hypotheses—and less so with behavioral intentions? Would so many subjects need to rationalize such innocent behavior? And where reinforcement was programmed alike for all, why should it happen to strengthen automatically some subjects' responses and also select their correct (or correlated) behavioral hypotheses? We might further assume that some unknown dispositions to both were correlated over subjects; and, of course, less so than for dispositions to automatic strengthening and to selection of behavioral intentions, and more so than for dispositions to automatic strengthening and to reinforcement hypotheses. (An analogous problem is presented by the correlation of reports and response selection within subjects but over responses. Levin [1961] and Spielberger, Levin, & Shepard [1962] found that when I and We are both reinforced and the subject selects only one pronoun, he reports awareness only of the pronoun he selects. To maintain the interpretation of automatic strengthening and common selection in this case, we should now have to assume some correlation, over *responses,* of dispositions to automatic strengthening and to representation in awareness.)

In short, whether we augment a theory of automatic strengthening with assumptions of suggestion, rationalization, emergence, or common selection, we are left to find still more assumptions that will explain the distinct pattern of relations among response selection and levels of RH, BH, and BI reports. Even if there should be assumptions that will resolve these questions, the relation of negatively correlated reports to avoidance of a reinforced response would be left for another theory—as would the effects of instruction. There would seem to be some advantage in a set of common hypotheses that appear to account for all of the findings fairly well and also bring the common relation of report to performance and of instructions to performance within the same formulation. Moreover, with that network of hypotheses in mind we can have a way of approaching a number of rather difficult problems that are now, with human subjects, less comfortably put aside.

Summary and conclusions

In the research summarized here we repeatedly find no evidence of verbal operant conditioning without awareness—using report of a correct or correlated hypothesis as the indicator of awareness and a tone, "Umhmm," "Good," or avoidance of electric shock as the consequence. Certainly it is possible that with somewhat different conditions—perhaps longer series of trials, more potent reinforcers, or less figural response classes—we would have found it. But if this kind of learning or conditioning without awareness is to have the social generality commonly imputed to it (as by Dollard and Miller, 1950, for example) it seems likely that we would have found it in some of these experiments. Set against this is the repeated finding that subjects who report certain forms of awareness, or are informed in terms cognate with these forms, differ significantly—and usually dramatically—from controls.

I have outlined a network of propositions encompassing instructions, hypotheses, intentions, private reports, habits, and response selection. If this presumption is justified at all, it is in the usefulness of that network. It does provide a way of handling the subjects' reports by treating report validity as an inductively confirmable hypothesis within the network. It provides a conception of awareness that relates awareness to response selection. And it specifies a meaning of hypotheses and intentions that is close to usage in informal theory and empirical by virtue of the connections of the network with experimental variables. Furthermore, the theory predicts and interprets our distinct pattern of findings: the relation of response selection to report of a correct or correlated hypothesis or intention; the relation of selection of a correct response to levels of report and levels of instruction, when those levels are based on estimates of parameters of response correlation; the intrinsic relations of levels of BH (behavioral hypotheses) and BI (behavioral interactions) reports, and of BH and RH (reinforcement hypotheses) reports, while there is none for BI and RH reports; and the intrinsic relation of levels of report of behavioral intention, only, to response selection when the other two report variables are statistically controlled. What appears to be the expression of habit in transfer without awareness is also comprehended by the theory, though we have still to establish its hypothesized antecedents.

Whatever may be our abstract misgivings about premature theorizing, the more fundamental questions the literature has raised are theoretical questions. Even to ask about verbal control and report validity, as against automatic strengthening, commits us to a logic of competing theories. The theoretical network that I have outlined merely states some of the cruder and more obvious hypotheses, perhaps a base from which the investigation of verbal control might be expanded. The inevitable incompleteness of the network, and of course of our work, is emphasized by the questions the network raises—for example, the locus of effect of variables such as drive, incentive, and numerous personal and interpersonal variables. But even when we ask whether those effects are voluntary or involuntary, we may phrase the questions within this network of hypotheses, and if they should be experimentally answerable, this too may have been useful.

References

Adams, J.   Laboratory studies of behavior without awareness.   *Psychol. Bull.*, 1957, **54**, 383-405.

Azrin, W. M., Holz, W., Ulrich, R., and Goldiamond, I.   The control of the content of conversation through reinforcement.   *J. exp. anal. Behav.*, 1961, 4, 25-30.

Bechtoldt, H. P.   Construct validity: A critique.   *Amer. Psychologist*, 1959, 14, 619-629.

Bergman, G.   The logic of psychological concepts.   *Phil. Sci.*, 1951, 18, 93-110.

Blaufarb, H. The relation of experimenter status and achievement imagery to the conditioning of verbal behavior.   Unpublished Ph.D. thesis, Univer. of Illinois, 1960.

Bridgman, P. W.   *The logic of modern physics.*   New York: Macmillan, 1927.

Campbell, D. T., & Fiske, D. W.   Convergent and discriminant validation by the multi-trait-multimethod matrix.   *Psychol. Bull.*, 1959, 56, 81-105.

Carnap, R.   The methodological character of theoretical concepts.   In H. Feigl and M. Scriven (Eds.), *The foundations of science and the concepts of psychology and psychoanalysis.*   Minneapolis: Univer. Minn. Press, 1956, pp. 38-76.

Cronbach, L. J., & Meehl, P. E.   Construct validity in psychological test.   *Psychol. Bull.*, 1955, 52, 281-302.

Dollard, J., & Miller, N.   *Personality and psychotherapy.*   New York: McGraw-Hill, 1950.

Dulany, D. E.   Reinforcement of verbal behavior.   Final report of research supported by National Science Foundation Grant G-4461, 1960.

Dulany, D. E.   Hypotheses and habits in verbal "operant conditioning."   *J. abnorm. soc. Psychol.*, 1961, 63, 251-263.

Eriksen, C. W.   Discrimination and learning without awareness: A methodological survey and evaluation.   *Psychol. Rev.*, 1960, 67, 279-300.

Feigl, H.   Some major issues and developments in the philosophy of science of logical empiricism.   In H. Feigl and M. Scriven (Eds.), *The foundations of science and the concepts of psychology and psychoanalysis.*   Minneapolis: Univer. Minn. Press, 1956, pp. 3-37.

Floden, C. R.   An attempt at operant verbal conditioning using verbal reinforcement.   Unpublished M.A. thesis, Univer. of Illinois, 1959.

Garner, W. R., Hake, H. W., & Eriksen, C. W.   Operationism and the concept of perception.   *Psychol. Rev.*, 1956, 63, 149-159.

Gibson, J. J.   A critical review of the concept of set in contemporary experimental psychology.   *Psychol. Bull.*, 1941, 38, 781-817.

Greenspoon, J.   The reinforcing effect of two spoken sounds on the frequency of two responses.   *Amer. J. Psychol.*, 1955, 68, 409-416.

Hempel, C. G.   *Fundamentals of concept formation in empirical science.*   Chicago: Univer. of Chicago Press, 1952.

Hilgard, E. R., & Marquis, D. G.   *Conditioning and learning.*   New York: Century, 1940.

Kimble, G.   *Hilgard and Marquis' Conditioning and learning.*   (2nd. ed.)   New York: Appleton, Century, Crofts, 1961.

Komosa, G. Relation between verbal response learning and the subject's perception of himself and the experimenter. Unpublished A.B. thesis, Univer. of Illinois, 1958.

Krasner, L. Studies of the conditioning of verbal behavior. *Psychol. Bull.,* 1958, 55, 148-171.

Levin, S. M. The effects of awareness on verbal conditioning. *J. exp. Psychol.,* 1961, 61, 67-75.

Luria, A. R. The role of speech in the regulation of normal and abnormal behavior. U. S. Dept. of Health, Education, and Welfare, 1960.

Matarazzo, J. D., Saslow, G., & Pareis, N. E. Verbal conditioning of two response classes: Some methodological considerations. *J. abnorm. soc. Psychol.,* 1960, 61, 190-206.

Miller, G. A., Galanter, E., & Pribram, K. H. *Plans and the structure of behavior.* New York: Holt, Dryden, 1960.

Oltman, P. K. Reported hypotheses and intentions in motor operant conditioning. Unpublished A.B. thesis, Univer. of Illinois, 1960.

Peak, H. An evaluation of the concepts of reflex and voluntary action. *Psychol. Rev.,* 1933, 40, 71-89.

Postman, L., & Sassenrath, J. The automatic action of verbal rewards and punishments. *J. gen. Psychol.,* 1961, 65, 109-136.

Salzinger, Kurt. Experimental manipulation of verbal behavior: A review. *J. gen. Psychol.,* 1959, 61, 65-94.

Sapolsky, A. Effect of interpersonal relationships upon verbal conditioning. *J. abnorm. soc. Psychol.,* 1960, 60, 241-246.

Sarason, I. G. Interrelationships among individual difference variables, behavior in psychotherapy, and verbal conditioning. *J. abnorm. soc. Psychol.,* 56, 1958, 339-395.

Skinner, B. F. *Verbal behavior.* New York: Appleton-Century-Crofts, 1938.

Skinner, B. F. *Science and human behavior.* New York: Macmillan, 1953.

Skinner, B. F. *Verbal behavior.* New York: Appleton-Century-Crofts, 1957.

Spielberger, C. D., Levin, S. M., & Shepard, Mary C. The effects of awareness and attitude toward the reinforcement on the operant conditioning of verbal behavior. *J. Pers.,* 1962, 30, 106-121.

Taffel, C. Anxiety and the conditioning of verbal behavior. *J. abnorm. soc. Psychol.,* 1955, 51, 496-502.

Tatz, S. J. Symbolic activity in "learning without awareness." *Amer. J. Psychol.,* 1960, 73, 239-247.

Tuite, M. H. On the relation of verbalization to the effect of verbal reinforcement. Unpublished A.B. thesis, Univer. of Illinois, 1960.

Uzgiris, Ina C. Awareness and conditioning of verbal behavior. Unpublished M.A. thesis, Univer. of Illinois, 1960.

Verplanck, W. S. The operant, from rat to man: An introduction to some recent experiments on human behavior. *Transactions of the New York Academy of Sciences,* 1955, 17, 594-601.

Zaporozhets, A. V. Origin and development of conscious control of movements in man. From *Problems of Psychology,* 1958, 4, 24-36. In *The central nervous system and behavior,* Selected translations from the Russian Medical Literature, U. S. Public Health Service, 1959, pp. 1005-1023.

Unaware of where's awareness: Some verbal operants—notates, monents, and notants

William S. Verplanck, *University of Maryland*

For some years now, problems of "learning without awareness" have arisen in a number of contexts; they have created a theoretical —and sometimes an experimental—fuss. Willy-nilly, those who investigate human operant behavior sooner or later are among those involved, whether they have leaped, slipped, or been dragged into the fray. These seem to be the avenues by which participants enter into scientific controversies, as well as into barroom brawls.

The courses of development of these two kinds of controversy are rather similar. They show a certain orderliness. In both, as the dispute rises in heat, and the blows—or experiments—get exchanged at higher rates, the original issue tends to get lost, if there was one to begin with. In the present case, the issue sum-marizes itself in "You can't," "I can," in progressively stronger inflections. Just what can or cannot be done either has been omitted, or repeatedly redefined, as the controversy has extended itself. It is not surprising that seemingly contradictory results turn up. To this writer, the present dispute, which seems to have something to do with the subject's ability to state experimental contingencies, is a regrettable one. As it has developed it seems to have led to the performance of experiments on inappropriate forms of behavior, and to a proliferation of speculative theory.

By inappropriate forms of behavior, I mean this: the experi-ments that have been—by now—repeated over and over with only minor modifications are those that have confounded at least two questions, the identification of response[1] classes and the sta-bility (habituability) of reinforcers. "Saying plural nouns," "con-structing sentences in the first person," "Mm-hmm," and "Good"

---

[1] For the usage of the terms *response* and *stimulus,* see stimulus (3) in the writer's glossary (Verplanck, 1957). See also Stimulus III (Verplanck, 1954); and Gibson (1960).

may serve to demonstrate the occurrence of operant conditioning, but they are not necessarily the best choices for experiments on other problems. Statements about whether or not operant conditioning occurs must depend upon the changes in behavior that occur with reinforcement and its withdrawal, and not upon anything the subject may have to say about it. (It should also be superfluous to point out that the terms "voluntary" and "operant" refer, by and large, to the same behaviors.) Many psychologists, in pursuing thought along these lines, seem to have tended to adopt ever more subtle (but not stringent) definitions of "awareness" and to have introduced theory in inverse proportion to the clarity of their experimental findings. Some seem to believe that if they can somehow demonstrate something that can be tagged with the label "awareness," they have in some sense found an "explanation" for the orderliness of human conditioning.

One would not express discomfort with this state of affairs if it were not for the fact that this seems, at least to the writer, the wrong time to attempt to use "awareness" as explanatory, or descriptive, of much of anything. The fact is, very little is suggested as to how "awareness," however it may have been defined, can or does control or affect behavior in the first place. Statements about "awareness" as prerequisite to learning have shown little, if any, experimental unity, and the word seems to have become a label indicating an explanatory dead end. However the issues as they have thus far been stated were resolved, little new information would be added.

The word seems to be associated with a rather special kind of phenomenological approach to behavior. While this may seem somewhat heretical to those phenomenologically oriented, to the writer it has always seemed that when the experimental facts get established, their phenomenological aspects seem to take care of themselves.

Some years ago, E. J. Green (1955) remarked that each of his subjects in a discrimination experiment could figure out its correct basis only once. The writer had made much the same observation during human conditioning (Verplanck, 1956). In the latter experiments, many subjects have a good deal to say while being conditioned; some of what they say is to the point. That is, some of it corresponds to the experimenter's rules in conditioning the sub-

ject. Both these observations related rather directly to subjects'
behavior in a number of exploratory experiments on discrimination
and "concept-formation" that the writer had been doing. In these,
while seeming to behave in conformity with continuity theory, the
subjects always did a lot of "hypothesizing" (again, some of it to
the point) à la the Tolman-Krechevsky school. Even the writer,
resent it though he may (as a Spencian incrementalist at the time),
found that he "hypothesized" when serving as a subject. Self-
observation, however, yielded few clues as to what was going on.

The common link seemed to be this: in all cases, the subject
could come across the correct rule, the "solution," only once in
any experiment. Only once could Green's subjects catch on to the
critical dots that were correlated with reinforcement. Only once
could the conditioning subjects "catch on" that "touching the nose
with the right forefinger" produced a point. Only once could
subjects figure out that pictures of "objects that can be used in
transport" were to be put in the pile on the right. The correct
rule, once said, hung on, the problem was solved (ten successive
correct choices), and the experiment terminated.

The "aha" that came is this: in operant conditioning of rats
and pigeons, too, the subject is observed to "solve the problem"
only once. Thereafter he "applies the solution." In shaping
bar-pressing or key-pressing, the skilled experimenter finds very
quickly that he is dealing with a one-trial event. The first bar-
press that yields the click of food dropping into the magazine, and
then the rat's quick dive toward it (a Guthrian affair), is followed
in most cases by another bar-press, after an interresponse time that
is no greater than those that are later recorded after 10 or 100
reinforcements. Where this does not occur, it seems that the experimenter, not the rat, made the mistake. We may look back
at Estes' paper on conditioning (Estes, 1950). To attain a clear-
cut incremental process in bar-pressing, he found it necessary to
introduce a second bar; gradual changes in pressing bar 1 occurred
while extinction to bar 2 was going on. One might put it this
way: incremental processes in conditioning seem always to involve extinction, either of the response itself to stimuli other than
the one the experimenter has chosen, or of a competing response.
With proper experimental control, operant conditioning is a "once"
affair; subsequent reinforcements serve primarily to maintain it

at strength, and to develop resistance to extinction, which might be characterized as "reluctance to give up the solution." At the time these considerations were asserting themselves, the writer was busy defining "response" for a glossary, and was struck both by the restrictions that this empirical definition placed on the kind of behavioral events to which the term applied and by the extraordinary range of new behaviors which could experimentally prove to be responses, behaving, under discriminative and reinforcing stimuli, in a simple manner.

All this suggested an approach to some of the problems raised by human behavior, and especially by verbal concepts. Let experimental work seek to establish directly how the verbal behavior occurring in an experiment is related to the other behaviors that occur. Verbal behaviors, if overt, meet the behaviorist's demands for experimental data, and while they can hardly be expected to bear a one-to-one relationship with concepts of "awareness," "hypotheses," "mediators," and the like used by others, there can be no dispute that they have something to do with at least part of what may be meant by "awareness." So, we sought to make a direct experimental attack upon the problem of how verbal behavior acts under the effect of various environmental conditions, and how it in turn is related to the motor behaviors with which it is, at least linguistically, associated. Just how closely such verbal behaviors may relate to "awareness" must be left to those who are surer than I of what is referred to by the word.

Specifically, we undertook to investigate the "rules"[2] that subjects say to themselves, and try out in various experimental problems. So long as these are allowed to remain covert, the experimenter forfeits the opportunity to exert direct experimental control over them. If they are made overt, the experimenter can directly subject them to environmental contingencies, as he can other behaviors. The ways in which they are controlled by antecedent or consequent stimuli can be determined by straightforward and simple experimental methods. We should be able to de-

[2] Since this paper was given, a monograph (Shepard, Hovland, & Jenkins, 1961) has appeared in which the results of experiments on much more complex problems of the same class are reported. It is encouraging to note that data were gathered on the rules—the notants—that subjects eventually came up with. But no effort was made to determine experimentally their origin, and their history through differential reinforcement. It is the behavior of such "rules" that this paper deals with.

termine how they occur in response to environmental events, how they serve as discriminative stimuli for other behaviors, and how they alter in strength with reinforcement.

Our first guess was that overt verbal statements of "rules" would prove to be simple operant behaviors, conditionable as are other operants. Preliminary experimentation based on this proposition led to methods that have since been further developed. The first method is a simple one: it requires the subject in a "concept-formation" card-sorting experiment to state aloud, on each presentation of a stimulus-object, the "rule" that he is following in trying to get as many cards as possible correctly placed to right or left. In this situation, where many different possible rules may apply, the experimenter is able to make social reinforcement ("Right" or "Wrong") contingent either upon the particular statement made by the subject, or upon the behavior that the statement instructed the subject to perform. In either case, he may deliver it *after* the placement.

Preliminary experiments determined the selection of the stimulus material and the problem. Stimulus materials which permit the experimenter to choose any one of an almost unlimited number of possible "solutions" proved indispensable. The experimenter must be free to change the "solution" of any problem in midstream—he must be able to make wrong what was previously right, and right what was wrong. He must have far more latitude than provided by, say, the Weigl cards. Second, the material must not require the acquisition of names (the acquisition of a single new response to an arbitrary class of events; stated conversely, the acquisition of a new stimulus class. See Shepard *et al.,* 1962). Third, the behavior required should not press the subject's immediate memory span.

The dissociability of "rule" and behavior

The results of these experiments led us to choose as the first formal experiment one that seemed to place maximal demands on the proposition that subjects' "hypotheses" are simple operants. We (that is, Stuart Oskamp [1956] and the writer) chose to show that these would occur at a high relative frequency even under partial reinforcement, under conditions where we could also keep track of the behavior presumed to be controlled by them.

Stimulus materials consisted of a set of 110 children's "trading cards"[3]—backs of playing cards, each different from all the others. Single objects or figures were represented on 55 of these, and 55 had two or more objects pictured. The subjects' task was, given the cards one at a time, to place each either to the right or to the left. The instructions also told the subject that he could get all of them correctly placed. Three groups of college students were run. Members of all three groups, *P*, *P*H, and P*H*, received the instructions to place each card to either right or left. Two of the groups, *P*H and P*H*, received the further instruction to state on each trial the rule followed in attempting to get the card right, before placing it. The first group, *P*, and one of the latter two groups, *P*H, were told "Right" or "Wrong" on each trial according to whether the card was placed correctly. The third group, P*H*, was told "Right" or "Wrong," according to whether they had stated a specific version of the rule followed by the experimenter in reinforcing, regardless of where they placed the card. (In group designations, the italic indicates whether P [placement] or H ["hypothesis"] was reinforced.) For all groups, reinforcement with "Right" or "Wrong" was given only after the card was placed.

In order to assure that any experimental results obtained could not be accounted for in terms of partially correct hypotheses, only a limited subset of the rules that could produce consistently correct placements was positively reinforced in members of group P*H*. That is, we shaped a particular set. The rules differentially reinforced for group P*H* were all of the form: "Single (one) principal object (figure, design) to the right, two (more than one, several, two, three) principal objects (figures, designs) to the left." If the subject, in stating the rule, *named* the object or objects pictured, he was told "Wrong." He had to use an abstract term. Records

[3] The tremendous variety in trading cards, on which pictures and designs vary in innumerable dimensions, and which may be further varied, independent of their individuality, by presenting them to the subject upside down, sidewise, or the like, makes such procedures possible. There are an effectively infinite number of possible rules that the experimenter can follow in giving reinforcement, and among which he can shift, whether he is reinforcing moments or placements. Similarly, their variety permits the experimenter to select stimulus materials with considerable freedom and control, although never with the degree of control provided by "artificial" materials, such as the Weigl cards. This flexibility seems indispensable for finding the orderly behavior of our subjects.

were kept, trial by trial, both of placements, and, for groups PH and P*H*, of rules stated.

The procedure was this: acquisition trials were carried out as usual in this type of concept-formation experiment (continuous reinforcement of correct responses) until the subjects met the criterion of ten successive correct responses. Thereafter, with no change in instruction to the subject nor any other indication of an alteration in procedure, all subjects were placed on a partial reinforcement schedule, in which they were told "Wrong" following each incorrect response, and following four out of each successive ten *correct* responses (placements for P and PH; rule statements for P*H*). On the remaining 60 per cent of correct responses, they were told "Right." These positive reinforcements were given according to a predetermined randomized schedule.

This schedule places the correct rule-statement on partial positive reinforcement, and at the same time punishes incorrect rule-statement 100 per cent of the time. The strength of correct rule-statement will depend, then, on reinforcement by avoidance, on partial positive reinforcement, or on both. Any of these provides accrual of strength by conditioning processes.

Many statements that subjects in group PH could make would lead them to place the cards consistently in the correct pile (e.g., "one dog, belongs to the right," "two dancers go to the left"), but these were not reinforced, since they did not correspond with the rule-statement required by the experimenter. For members of group PH, if such "Wrong" statements were followed by placements consistent with them, they would be followed by reinforcement contingent on the correct placement.

The results of this experiment were clear. First, although the mean number of trials to criterion was smallest for group PH, such differences among groups were not reliable. Several subjects in this group first stated a correct rule following three or four consecutive correct placements. But our primary interest is in the behavior under partial reinforcement. Of the placements made by subjects in groups P and PH on reinforcement trials 51 through 100[4] following the ten trials in the criterion run, 60 per cent were

---

[4] Through the first 50 trials, the percentage correct drops from 100 per cent to an asymptotic value. The rate at which this occurs varies from subject to subject, evidently as a function of differences in the aversiveness of the socially presented "Wrong."

reinforced, and for *PH* 58.9 per cent of correct placements followed instances of the correct rule that were reinforced. The percentages of correct placements under partial reinforcement were, respectively, 71.2, 71.8, and 76.8, which differ significantly from chance (50 per cent), but not from one another. On the 23.2 per cent of the trials on which members of *PH* made incorrect placements, these subjects were reinforced 43.9 per cent of the time; that is, with 4 of every 10 incorrect placements, they stated the correct rule, the one for whose statement they were being reinforced. More striking are the percentages of trials on which (*a*) the correct rule, (*b*) rules that were incorrect, but yielded correct placements, (*c*) rules that related to the objects pictured, rather than to other features of the stimulus material (borders, colors, realism, and the like), were stated by members of *PH* and *PH*, the two groups giving the rules on each trial. These are summarized in Table 1.

Table 1. Percentages of trials 51-100 on which members of groups PH and PH stated each of four categories of rules

Category of rule stated	Group PH	Group PH
(1) Correct rule......................	30.2	92.2
(2) Other version of rule that would yield correct placement consistently..........	18.2	2.0
(3) Incorrect rules that named object depicted......................	17.2	0.2
(4) All others........................	34.4	5.6

The data of the table indicate clearly that the rule that has been, and continues to be differentially reinforced, occurs at high relative frequency. Its relative frequency is higher than that of the behavior it is presumed to control. Although *PH* subjects state the correct rule on 92.2 per cent (and one or another version of it on 94.2 per cent) of the trials, they place the cards correctly on only 76.8 per cent of the trials. In other words, they do not place the card where they say they are going to on 17.4 per cent of the trials. Group *PH*, however, states the correct rule, or a version of it, on 48.4 per cent of the trials, but places the cards correctly on 71.8 per cent—a discrepancy of 23.4 per cent in the other direction. The rule-statement, and the behavior for which it is presumably a discriminative stimulus, have been dissociated by manipulating their contingencies of reinforcement.

In a later experiment by Rilling (1962) on the reinforcing properties of "Right" and "Wrong," one group underwent an experimental procedure which replicated that of group *PH*. He obtained results almost identical with those of Oskamp (1956): on 72.8 per cent of the trials, the placement was correct; on only 57.1 per cent of the trials was any version of the experimentally correct rule given.

The results may be summarized as follows: under partial reinforcement, the statement of a specific rule retains considerable strength, as do simple operants. The strength is, in fact, greater than that of the behavior that the rule is presumed to control—here, the placement of a card. Where reinforcement is contingent on placement, a higher percentage of correct placements occurs than can be accounted for by correct rules. Experimentally, the subject's rules, his "hypotheses," can be dissociated to a degree from the behaviors that they are presumed to direct. He does not carry out his intentions.

The monent

In fairness both to theorists, and to the conceptual system within which this experiment was done, it is now necessary to introduce a term for these "statements-of-a-rule" by our subjects. They must be distinguished from the "hypotheses" referred to in many theories and from the rules followed by the experimenter in conducting the experiments. The term chosen is "monent," derived from a Latin verb meaning "advising, guiding, or directing," and it is "monents" that now become subject to a number of experiments aimed at determining further how subject's verbal behavior acts in controlling other of his behaviors. The outcome of this experiment leads, also, to further methods of investigating such verbal behaviors, and hence to data that have shown their status as operants, their discriminative stimuli, and the kinds of events that reinforce them. For clarity of exposition, we will reserve the words "rule" and "principle," for the rules followed by the experimenter. Let me summarize very briefly a variety of experiments, in the approximate order in which they were done, with a brief account of the immediate context in which they were performed. All of them are based upon the experimental method of shifting the basis of reinforcement from monent to monent, from monent to placement according to one or another rule, from placement to placement, and back again.

A. *Extinction and recovery*. In order to determine how monents behave under extinction, we performed a number of experiments using the same stimulus materials, the same set of instructions as those given to groups *P*H and **P***H*, and the same general method.[5]

A simple demonstration comes when one gives the subject instructions to state the rule he is trying before each placement, and then tells him "Wrong" on every trial. Latencies of monents increase progressively, more and more improbable monents occur when they are finally given ("can be used to carry opium" is the writer's favorite), and finally the subject gives up—"I can't think of anything else"; "my mind's a blank," and so on. Only very rarely does a subject come up with the one paradoxically reinforceable monent: "*Anything* I say is going to be wrong!"

Extinction with spontaneous recovery occurs when the experimenter delivers reinforcement according to the following rules: reinforce five consecutive times the second monent stated by the subject (i.e., the monent first stated by the subject on the second trial); extinguish this monent thereafter, but give five consecutive reinforcements to the second new monent given after the last instance of the first reinforced monent. Repeat this shift in reinforcement two more times until each of four different monents has received five consecutive reinforcements, then shift to reinforcement of placement according to a rule that does not correspond with any of subject's monents. Under these conditions, subjects will eventually reach the criterion of 100 per cent correct placement, but the monents they state typically resemble closely

---

[5] Many of these effects can be obscured by averaging the data of subjects. It is the individual subject whose behavior is orderly. Combining the data of many subjects serves not only to force discontinuous data into a guise of continuity, but it also yields a degree of variability that leads one to seek "significance" by placing more and more subjects in each group, rendering it still less likely that one will either observe carefully the behavior of any one individual or sharpen up the experimental design. Subjects *do* differ from one another, and in ways that make group data treacherous.

the initially reinforced four. These recur, to be re-extinguished and again to recover spontaneously. The subject often is never able to state the rule followed by the experimenter in reinforcing placements, even though he reaches 100 per cent correct. Under these conditions, subjects may take several hundred trials to reach solution.

B. *The monent as a chain of responses.* The protocols of this and of similar experiments show that the monent is a chain composed of two responses, made up of a word or phrase descriptive of the card, the "notate," linked to an instruction, the "predocent" such as "put to the right," or "goes to the right." A notate may not recur after a single unreinforced occurrence. If the subject says "people go to the right" and gets no reinforcement, he is not likely to try "people go to the left"; he is more likely to say something such as "cards with blue go to the right." The two parts of the monent thus may be separated; their initial strengths differ greatly, as does their resistance to extinction.

A "notate" (Latin—roughly translatable as "what has been observed") is defined as follows: any word or phrase given in response to a stimulus or to an object incorporating stimuli. Notates can be further characterized as "descriptions," "associations," "discriminated responses," "descriptive characteristics," "categories," or even "verbal percepts." Notates are stimulus-controlled and are symbolic of one or another feature of the stimulus. They are synonymous, then, with Skinner's (1957) "tact."

The second part, "put to the right," "goes to left" termed the "predocent" (roughly "instructing beforehand"), is defined as a verbal response that is an S^D for motor behavior. (One might expect that there would be a third member of the chain, "is correct." Such occur very rarely.)

C. *Some response equivalences, and lack of them.* In some experiments, subjects have been permitted to say "same." If, after a series of "sames," the subject is asked what "same" means, he gives the monent last stated. That is, the subject's "same" can be believed, and reinforcing "same" gives results identical, insofar as can be determined, with those obtained by reinforcing the last previously stated monent itself. Another effect should be noted:

reinforcing "borders go to the left" is *ordinarily* equivalent to reinforcing "nonborders go to the right." Under some circumstances in placement reinforcement, which we would hesitate to try to characterize as yet, the two may be dissociated, and the subject may systematically say, "borders to the left," and "animals to the right," depending on the stimulus card presented. That is, monents may adventitiously become differentially reinforced with respect to stimuli. The effects of the adventitious reinforcement of "borders" when presented with cards having borders are not incompatible with those of the adventitious reinforcement of "animals" to cards with animals, and to cards with both borders and animals.

Again under circumstances that have not yet been determined, subjects may show a perfect discrimination for placements to the right, and show no discrimination of placements to the left, without respect to the strength of any monent. In these cases, some cards that belong on the right are being put to the left, and the S^D for right placement has not yet become identical to that feature of the stimulus cards which the experimenter has chosen. For the subject, the S^D is a subclass of the stimulus the experimenter has chosen.

D. *The discrimination process: extinction of placements to S^Δ.* Further analyses were made on the data obtained on individual subjects in groups P and *PH* of the initial experiment, and on subjects in other experiments following similar procedures. In these, cumulative frequencies of placements to the right are plotted as a function of cumulative instances of S^D (i.e., the class of cards that belong on the right according to the experimenter's rule) and of S^Δ for this response. A similar pair of curves is plotted for placements to the left. These curves show that incorrect card placements (the two S^Δ-R curves) fall off in extinction curves. Under *PH* instructions, the correct monent tends to occur for many subjects only after considerable extinction has taken place. When this occurs, the extinction process is short-circuited out, and the extinction curve takes a slope of zero at once. But considerable (and recoverable) resistance to extinction for either R in the presence of their S^Δ's remains, to reveal itself in "careless errors."

These results emphasize the fact that monents are not discriminated, but, once they occur correctly, may be reinforced on every trial thereafter, whereas placements to the right or to the left can be reinforced only when their discriminative stimuli (cards that go to right and to left respectively) are presented. Placements seem governed by Spencian laws, based on differential reinforcement with respect to two sets of stimuli, that is, with reinforcement of correct and nonreinforcement of incorrect responses with respect to their stimuli. The correct monent, by contrast, as in simple operant conditioning, is reinforced on every trial, irrespective of the particular stimulus presented, and single reinforcements yield immediate repetitions. Both continuity and noncontinuity theories are substantially correct—but for different behaviors. However, unless reinforcement of monents is experimentally distinguished from that of placements, the correct monent will "take over" as soon as it occurs, and will obscure the gradual development of a discrimination.

E. *Differential reinforcement of monents.* It should be possible to place monents under discriminative control by making reinforcement of a particular monent contingent upon the presence of a particular discriminative stimulus. Thus, under S^D (as experimenter leaning forward or the card presented sidewise) "people to the right, nonpeople to the left" can be reinforced, and under S^Δ (experimenter sitting up straight or the card presented straight up and down) "cards with borders go to the right, nonborders to the left." (This is evidently the "conditional hypothesis.") Experiments of this sort were done, and, the expected discrimination curves for the monents were found.

F. *Manipulability of availability of monents.* When subjects are used in a series of experiments, with the reinforced monent varied from time to time, there are large transfer effects. An initially improbable monent may appear first in a new experiment, if it has been reinforced in an earlier one. Subject's repertory of monents, and their relative probabilities, may be manipulated over a wide range ("salience").

G. *Covert monents.* It should be emphasized that no assertion has been made that the spoken monent is the only verbal behavior involved. Subjects show many signs of covert verbal behavior, and much of this becomes overt when the experimenter asks questions. The subjects' answers often yield additional notates and monents different from what was given aloud, or give elaborated versions of the overt one: "I was wondering if it had something to do with alternate piles, too," or "It may be a particular *kind* of people." These previously unstated monents (where the subject is not following the experimenter's instruction to him) may pick up a few reinforcements adventitiously.

The final experiments of this series deal with covert monents directly.

H. *Conditioning of covert monents, as superstitions.* An experiment was designed to determine whether a covert event that corresponds in its behavior with the monent occurs. Subjects, run together in sets of five before an audience, have been given the following instructions: "You will be shown a series of pictures. Following a simple rule, some of them are plusses, and some minuses. Your job is to find the rule that makes each card a plus or a minus. On each trial, write in your data book whether you think the picture is a plus or a minus, and you will be told whether you are right or wrong each time. When you think you know what the rule is, put a check next to your answer on that trial. When you are certain what the rule is, put a double check." The subjects were then individually reinforced according to an arbitrary prearranged schedule, independent of their overt response, although the individuals delivering the reinforcements went through the motions of looking at them, before saying "Right" or "Wrong."

On trials 1, 3, 4, and 7, all subjects were told "Wrong." On all other trials through trial 30, all subjects were told "Right." Over the next 12 trials (31-42), one of each set of five subjects was told "Wrong" once, another 3 times, another 6 times, another 9 times. On the other trials, all were told "Right." In each set, one control subject remained on continuous reinforcement, that is, he was told "Right" on every trial past 7. All subjects were then continuously reinforced for a further 28 trials (to a total of 70). At the end, the subjects were asked to write down the rule that was correct, and how sure they were of it, and, if the rule changed, to write down the second rule, and how sure they were of it. This procedure has been replicated a number of times.

In this procedure, then, reinforcements occur—are "shot in"—at times when a moment should have occurred covertly, but the reinforcement was independent of what the moment might be. Moments could be conditioned, then, as "superstitions." The results indicated that covert moments occur, and that they behave under reinforcement as do overt ones.

1. Every subject reported at least one rule of which he was "certain" or "very sure." The relative frequencies of the moments that were conditioned correspond with those observed of overt moments before differential reinforcement (animals, people, borders, realistic, upside down, single vs. plural, and the like).

2. For the 18 subjects who followed the instruction to check and double check, a median of four consecutive reinforcements (range 1-14) preceded the trial on which they reported that they "thought they knew what the rule was," and a median of five more reinforcements (range 3-22) made them "certain" or "very sure." Of those subjected to partial reinforcement through trials 31-42 an insufficient number of subjects made checks, so that no results can be reported.

3. A single nonreinforcement seldom extinguishes or alters the correct moment after it has been on continuous reinforcement for some time. In general, the greater the number of nonreinforcements, the more different the second covert moment from the first. (Table 2)

Table 2. Number of changes in moments reported as a function of number of nonreinforcements through trials 31-42. $(N = 25)$

	Group	A	B	C	D	E
	No. "Wrongs" trials 31-42	0	1	3	6	9
Kind of change	None	5	2	1	1[a]	0
	Minor change[b]	0	3	3	2	2
	Complete change[c]	0	0	1	2	3

[a] The subject wrote: "red in background, +. Changed in middle (of series), and went back to original."

[b] Minor changes include (a) simple reversals, additions (original: "persons = +; then persons with horses = +"), contractions (original: living things +, then animals and flowers +), expansions (original: "animals negative" to "live negative").

[c] Complete changes: no relationship between first moment and second, e.g., "borders +, to animals +," and "animals and humans +," to "photos."

4. At the end of the series of 70 cards, every one of the 25 subjects reported being certain of the first rule. Every subject who reported a change in the rule, was either "sure" or "pretty sure" of the second rule as well.

We may state with confidence that monents occur covertly, and that they are then subject to the same laws of reinforcement as when they are overt.

In all these experiments, the behavior of individual subjects was orderly to a high degree; subject's "thinking" came under experimenter's control in very much the way the behavior of a rat does when a response is being shaped. On the other hand, questioning a subject at the end of these experiments on what he was doing, or what he thought was going on, or how he solved the problem, yields a good deal of verbal behavior that usually corresponds poorly with what the subject had in fact been doing, or how frequently he had been reinforced. It reflects very seldom the environmental variables whose control led this subject to behave as other subjects do under the same procedure. What the subject answers to such questions seems to be most closely related to his behavior over the few trials immediately prior to the questioning, and suggests a short-range "immediate memory." Rationalizing, not reasoning, seems to be the appropriate term. The statements recall the flavor of the introspective protocols given by subjects in the functionalists' experiments at the beginning of the century. One can hear and see what led Watson to behaviorism.

The notant

In the preceding experiments, the experimenter was limited by the fact that he had to keep track of, and record, two kinds of behavior—the monent, and either card-placement, or writing + or —. Moreover, in delivering reinforcement, there was inevitably the ambiguity that both placement and monent could be reinforced on any one trial (the ambiguity is evident to remarkably few subjects). A new procedure was therefore developed that eliminated one of the two behaviors, and hence the ambiguity. It enabled us to study the verbal behavior alone.

The subject is presented with two side-by-side piles of cards, picture side down. These have previously been sorted by the ex-

perimenter according to some rule or sequence of rules. The
instructions are:

All the cards on the right differ, in a systematic way, that is, in the same
way, from all the cards on the left. Your job is to turn the cards over, a
pair at a time, and for each pair tell me the rule that you think distinguishes
all the ones on the right from all the ones on the left. I'll tell you
whether you are right or wrong.

By stacking the cards, the experimenter can arrange for several
rules to apply successively for fixed numbers of trials, thus providing the experimental conditions for extinction, counterconditioning, and the like.

A. *The notant: a chain of notates.* As with the moment, the
verbal behaviors, such as "cards with blue showing are on the
right," constitute a chain. As with the moments, a single nonreinforced occurrence usually eliminates the notate that is the first
member of the chain (and the subject does not say "cards with blue
are on the left"). From this fact, and from the fact that these
statements do not direct the subject to do anything further, it becomes necessary to distinguish between these chains and moments.
The first member of both, the discriminated verbal response to a
feature of the card "blues," "girls," "single object," is a notate.
The second member for moments is the "predocent," which "tells
the subject what to do." The class of verbal chains which state an
order in the environment are termed "notants." Their second
member is a "predicant," roughly translatable as "predicating
something about the environment," which is defined: a verbal
response to a notate, incorporating one or more other notates. The
notants in the present series of experiments are all of the sort—
"cards with borders are on the right," or "the right pile includes
all the bordered cards." "Border" and "right" are notate and
predicant respectively. The distinction between predicants and
other notates is an operational one: in these experiments, the stimuli for the predicants are presented on every trial. Those for other
notates need not be. The order in these chains is a matter determined largely by grammatical constraints and is often of no
great importance.

B. *Reinforcement by confirmation.* Initially, in these experiments the experimenter told the subject "Right" or "Wrong" fol-

lowing each notant. It soon became obvious that he need say nothing, and that the instructions could be changed. A notant shows the effects of reinforcement (one-trial change in response probability, and progressive-with-trials increments in resistance to extinction) as a function of the pair of stimuli presented to the subject on the following trial. If these stimuli elicit the notant given on the previous trial, they reinforce it. Such confirmation does not differ in its control over behavior from the social reinforcement "Right" and "Wrong," except quantitatively (*vide infra,* D). A confirmation is a reinforcing stimulus.

C. *Social vs. confirming reinforcement.* In some experiments on notants, the experimenter's "Rights" and "Wrongs" were given in contradiction to the reinforcement (by confirmation) given by the prearranged stacking of cards. These results are of importance in their own right, since striking individual differences in behavior are observed under these conditions. Some subjects under these conditions are controlled primarily by the social reinforcers, and others ignore these, and behave in conformity with the nonsocial confirmations.

D. *Relative availability of notants.* It was found possible to arrange the cards so that the availability of a given notate can be varied through a considerable range. This is done by arranging the cards in each of the two stacks in the order of ascending, or descending, probability that each will elicit the experimentally correct notate and no others. (E.g., border vs. no border is ordinarily a very difficult notate. However, it may be produced on trial number 1 by presenting the subject with a pair of cards about which there is nothing to say but "border," that is, two blank cards, one with a border.) The availability of a particular notate (which it will now be evident is almost identical with "concept") proves to be a simple function of the sequence of environmental events, and of the subject's previous experimental history. It is readily manipulatable by the experimenter.

E. *Extinction.* In these experiments, nonreinforcement of a notant can be carried out by one or another of a number of different operations. Let us say the notant is "flowers on the right, nonflowers on the left." Nonreinforcement of this notant can be associated with (*a*) systematically presenting a flower on the left, and no flower on the right, (*b*) systematically presenting no flowers at all, on either side, (*c*) systematically presenting flowers on both sides, and (*d*) having the two decks randomized with respect to flowers. All four procedures yield extinction curves, but it has not yet been determined whether the last three produce results different from one another. The first of the four counterconditions a new notant—"flowers on left" (cf. B, under monent). The notate continues to be reinforced; this corresponds with the "reversal shift," which seems to puzzle some theorists. With *b, c,* and *d,* the cards may be stacked so that a notant which incorporates a new notate can be conditioned.

F. *Counterconditioning.* In experiments where a new notant is subject to reinforcement as the previous one undergoes non-reinforcement, the extinguishing notate drops out for a time after only one or two nonreinforcements. The full characteristic extinction curve of the first is obtained only over a long series of trials during which the second notant occurs on each trial and is continuously reinforced. In this case, after a number of trials, subjects often tack on the extinguishing notate, as follows: if "cards with borders on the right" was reinforced, then extinguished, and "cards with blue showing on the right" then conditioned, subjects will, for example, say, when a card with both blue and a border appears on the right, "blue's on the right, and there's a border."

When the second notant undergoes extinction, still more instances of the first notant recur.

G. *Functions of the number of reinforcements.* Resistance to extinction, the number of unreinforced responses that occur after the termination of reinforcement, is a function of the number of regular reinforcements, here as in other conditioning. The subject's "certainty" is also a function of this number. After three or four consecutive reinforcements the subject is "pretty sure." After three or four more, he is "very sure," or "certain." Quantitative data of a sort may be obtained by asking the subject after each consecutive pair, or after a given number of regular reinforcements, how much he would be willing to bet that the next pair will conform with his notant.

H. *"Refining" the notant.*   When the experimenter has applied *two* principles in stacking the decks (cards with both borders and people to right, cards with neither borders nor people to left), many subjects, when one of the two notants has been conditioned and is under continuous reinforcement, will stick with the first one, unmodified.   A few subjects will, after a few more trials, emit the second notate as well, while the first is still under regular reinforcement.   Some of them speak of this as "refining my hypothesis."   Further experimental work is needed before we can determine under what conditions, and with what kinds of subjects, the latter highly adaptive behavior may be expected to occur.

I. *Notants and monents.*   In general, subjects arrive at an experimentally correct notant far more quickly than they do the experimentally correct monent.   This is true even when the difference in the number of cards presented per trial is taken into account.   This finding is consistent with the observation that bystanders watching a subject perform in a concept-formation experiment of the card-sorting type often get the concept more quickly than the subject himself.   The bystander is more effectively reinforced through observation of the cards that the subject has placed to right or left than the subject is by his own placement of them, and the differential social reinforcement he receives.

The notate, isolated

Concerned that the orderliness of the data obtained in these experiments might depend upon the particular stimulus material used, and on the instructions given by the experimenter, we sought a very different kind of material that could be used in similar experimental manipulations.   More particularly, we wished to deal with simple notates, unchained with other responses.   Such material has been used by Underwood (1957), who compiled lists of words illustrating concepts, and has done experimental work utilizing them.   As a result, we found ourselves in the area of word-association.   With the new material, a still further simplification of the experimental procedure proved not only possible, but desirable.

The experiments that follow are all based on the use of stimulus material that is made up of sets of words, ranging in number from 20 to 50.   Each set lists words that are the names of objects that have a single common property (objects that are round; rectangular; made of wood; made of paper, and so on).

On the basis of the work of Bousfield (e.g., 1953) and others, all the words of each list should have some measurable probability of eliciting the same word (the "concept") in a word-association experiment. "Orange," "wheel," and "clock-face" are all likely to yield "round." Initially, on a systematic basis, and now on an experimental one, these verbal responses have been identified as notates, and a concept is recognized as that class of stimuli all of which control the same notate. The name of the concept is given by the notate controlled by it.

The first experiment was the simple and obvious one, essentially replicating experiments that had already been done, but in a context, and using methodological details, that were new. The subjects were (individually) instructed as follows:

I will read you a list of words, all of which have something in common. Your job is to figure out what they all have in common. After each word, tell me what you think the common element or feature is, and I will tell you whether you are right or wrong.

In these experiments, the subject's behavior showed nothing that was not already familiar from the previous sets of experiments on notants.

As before, social reinforcement proved unnecessary; reinforcement by confirmation, given by the occurrence of a second word eliciting the same notate was similarly effective in (a) altering the probability of response after its first occurrence, (b) building resistance to extinction, (c) progressively building subject's certainty that he is "right," and (d) increasing his tendency to give the same notate to an initially ineffective or weak stimulus for it.

By arranging words in order of notate probabilities, the number of trials required by the subject to reach the correct notate can be varied up and down. Lists can be "stacked" as were the cards in the previous experiments.

Two classes of notates occasionally occur that are almost impossible to extinguish. The first is one so general that it is available as a response to almost any noun, e.g., "useful to humans." The other class of undisconfirmable notates are words that are inexact in their level of abstraction. One subject (a psychologist), given list A of the Appendix, and immediately thereafter list C in reverse order, gave "container" to the second stimulus word, "barrel." After the seven ensuing reinforcements of "container," "cigarette" yielded: "Container—contains air." The identical response was given to "wheel." Clock face "contains time." Objects thereafter contained food value, atoms, merit, and so on. A fascinating performance.

The effects produced when social and environmental reinforcement are given in contradiction to one another replicate those of the previous experiments on notants.

Altogether, these experiments confirmed the generalizations that had been arrived at, and rendered it most improbable that they were artifacts of the specific stimulus materials that had been used.

The use of word-lists suggested further and illuminating experiments.

A. *Notates and word associations.* When a subject is presented with a list of words, all members of one concept, but is instructed that this is a word-association test and that he is to say the first word he thinks of as soon as the word is pronounced, there seems to be a tendency for the correct notate to occur more often toward the end of the list. If, at the end of the list, the subject is told— "All the words I gave you were of the same sort; they were examples of the same kind of thing. Did you notice? What were they?", most subjects are immediately able to state the concept. (Subjects who cannot state it immediately do so after one or two words of the list when the list is now reread.) With no instructions to do so, they have "solved the problem"—which had not been stated. The mere presentation of a series of stimuli all of which control the same response alters the probability that the response will occur.

In an elaboration of this experiment, a group of 36 high-school students were given a "word-association test," in which four stimulus lists of 25 words each were given ("red," "footwear," "food," and "furniture"). Each word was spoken 6 times consecutively, at 4-second intervals: thus, up to six responses could be written to each (most subjects were able to give six consistently). After all the responses had been made, subjects were told that all the words on each of the four lists illustrated different concepts, and were asked what they were. Table 3 gives the results.

Table 3. Concepts reported following "word-association test" (N=36)

List 1 ("food")		List 2 ("footwear")		List 3 ("red")		List 4 ("furniture")	
food	32	clothing	7	accident	13	furniture	25
soft food	1	shoes,	7	(injury,		household,	2
gooey, (oozy)	2	footwear		violence,		articles	
none	1	travel	3	death)		comfort, relaxa-	4
		weather	2	red	10	tion	
		sports	2	color	3	home	2
		misc.	10	misc.	7	misc.	2
		none	5	none	5	none	1

These results show that subjects do indeed find concepts, even when not instructed to do so.

Examination of the data sheets reveals the word associations that compelled such correlated concepts. They show that the concept acquired by each subject is typically determined by his most frequent response, and that occurrence of a response increases its probability of occurring again. The "erroneous" concepts given by these subjects were produced by their most frequent responses.

This is best seen by the concept "accident, injury, violence, death" of the third list. The first word of this list was "blood," to which the great majority of college students give, as their first response, the word "red." The second word was "stop-light," the second most effective, for college students, in producing "red." When presented in this order to the 36 high school students in November, 1960, their first responses to "red" were given as in Table 4. When the subjects went on to "stop-light," they frequently produced "police car," "arrest," and related words. Having responded with words associated with crime, they tended to continue to do so. (Many "misheard" the word "radish" as "ravish," and responded accordingly.)

Table 4. Frequencies of notates to the word "blood" (N=36; high school students)

red	15	kill	1	accident	1	murder	1
Psycho	5	nurse	1	vampire	1	bring	1
cut(s)	4	drip	1	death	1	miss	1
fight	1	ugh	1	football	1		

It is not surprising that 13 of the 36 identified the concept, in retrospect, as Table 3 shows.

Quite clearly, the concept they "get" is the response they have just made most frequently. With "concept" instruction, this same list is gotten 100 per cent correctly in a matter of four or five trials.

General summary

Now, where are we?

We started with an explicit attempt to determine how the rules, the "hypotheses," which the subject "tries out" in operant-conditioning and concept-formation experiments, operate in controlling his behavior. We wound up, far afield, in word-association experiments. We started with a frank attempt to find out, irrespective of whether it is necessary for conditioning, how verbal behavior operates. We wound up with a new area where "incidental learning" takes place. The results of these experiments justify some tentative generalizations that may prove of use not only in bringing order into some of those areas of human learning where problems of "awareness" have arisen, but also in rendering problem-solving and similar complex behaviors amenable to experimental elucidation rather than theoretical elaboration.

I. When a discriminative stimulus is presented to a human subject, it produces, at different probabilities, a very broad variety of verbal responses. Each of these responses is termed a notate. Both the number and specific identity of those which are given overtly will be functions of the specific instructions that are given to the subject. Whether overt or covert, these responses are operants ("voluntary," if you will), and are subject to alteration in both probability of occurrence, and resistance to extinction.

II. The probability of occurrence of a given notate to one of its stimuli is a function of the numbers of preceding presentations of others of its stimuli. That is, the greater the number of a notate's stimuli that precede a specific one, the greater the probability that the notate will be given to that specific instance. This statement in itself may be no more than a rephrasing of a general law of stimulus summation; with continued presentation, a stimulus that is initially inadequate for a given response may elicit or release the response.

It follows, then, that the repetition of stimuli that initially do not produce a specific notate overtly, or (as revealed by questioning) covertly, will progressively tend to do so as they are presented following more and more stimuli which also have some low probability of yielding it.

(From this, it also follows that the introduction of a human subject into a given experimental situation will eventually lead him to respond systematically to initially "unnoticed" features of the environment. For example, if he gets "conditioned," he will almost necessarily notice it. Similarly, subjects will sooner or later start "making hypotheses" about features of the experimental setting and procedure which have been eliminated as controls over behavior by being held at constant values, or so the experimenter thinks.)

III. If a notate is stated on one trial, and if a stimulus for the same notate is given on the following trial, the notate is reinforced by confirmation, in the absence of any social reinforcement. A single reinforcement is sufficient to produce some resistance to extinction. If the notate is *correct,* with this one confirmation it reaches its maximal relative frequency with respect to instances of its stimulus class. It is "stuck in," and continues to be given so long as its stimuli occur.

IV. The effectiveness of reinforcement by confirmation is amplified many times by the experimenter's instructions to the subject, and by the subject's instructions to himself. What was initially a very weak reinforcer becomes, by instruction, an extremely strong one. The subject's certainty, his willingness to bet that he is right, is a simple function of the number of continuous reinforcements.

V. The statements about the environment made by a subject to himself are found to be of two sorts: those which simply describe the environment, but suggest no further behavior (notants), and those that provide him with discriminative stimuli for further behavior (moments). The latter are self-instructions, instructions of the subject to himself. They tell him what to do. Most of the time, he does it. Such moments may also be introduced to guide the subject's behavior by statement in the instructions.

The way to determine how a subject's behavior is guided by self-instructions is by the systematic experimental manipulation of instructions either to himself or from another. It is not wise to assume, as is usually done, that a subject will do what he is told to do, whether by himself or by another. Nor does it make sense to assume that, if we but knew the self-instruction, we would know "what the subject is really doing," or "what is controlling his behavior." Such relationships need to be experimentally established. It is encouraging that some aspects of this problem are now being explicitly investigated by Grant (1961), who has found not only some expected results, but some unexpected ones: apparently innocuous or inconsequential alterations in instructions can yield some large, unpredicted, and as yet cryptic quantitative changes in subjects' behavior.

VI. In most experiments on conditioning, problem-solving, and the like, the experimenter follows one rule throughout the experiment. From the foregoing it follows that the subject will almost always "find the rule," even when he has not necessarily been instructed to do so. It will hence be all but impossible, in a highly ordered laboratory situation, when the subject is "in an experiment," to preclude him from finding and stating the rules followed by the experimenter. He need hit the "right" rule only on one occasion for it to become subject to regular reinforcement. Only by devious means, as by distraction, can one expect to prevent a subject from verbally responding to the significant variables of the experiment.

VII. The subject's "certainty" that a rule is correct is a function of the number of continuous reinforcements it has had. Other schedules of reinforcement also increase resistance to extinction, but with another effect on "certainty." (As a subject on 60 per cent reinforcement in group PH said in explanation of his behavior, "Well, I knew it wasn't *exactly* right, but it was right *most* of the time, so I stuck with it.")

VIII. Reinforcement by confirmation is imprecise, not well-suited for shaping. The probability that the subject will get the exactly correct rule or principle will be determined by the sequence of stimuli given him, and only with precise control of these stimuli can such successful "solutions" be assured. Those experimenters who wish to shape up the correct notate, notant, or monent can do so, but when these verbal operants are allowed to occur covertly, picking up essentially uncontrolled reinforcements, some odd superstitions may occur.

IX. It would appear that whenever a monent is on continuous reinforcement, so that reinforcement is delivered alike to monent and the behavior it "directs," it will exert maximal control over the behavior for which it is the predocent.

X. Only by dissociating, in one way or another, the reinforcement of the monent from the reinforcement of the behavior controlled by the monent is it possible to show the nature of their relationship. Under partial reinforcement of the behavior, the strength of the correct monent becomes weaker than that of the behavior, and under partial reinforcement of the monent, its strength exceeds that of the behavior. The remaining resistance to extinction of the incorrect responses reveals itself in the form of occasional "errors."

Closing remarks

Where does this all leave us with respect to "awareness?"

"Awareness," as it has been described, seems to have been assigned no particular properties as a consequence of which differential behavior might be expected. It is used rather as a verbal magic that allows one to say that operant conditioning is not operant conditioning, because the subject was "aware." There are alternatives, however.

The burden of the experiments here reported seems to be this: Watson's "verbal reports," and Hunter's "SP-LR's" can be dealt with as can any other behavior. They do not need to be ignored, as they are by some. They do not need to be treated purely as reflecting some other process, some solely inferable state, whether "mediating process," "consciousness," or "awareness." As relevant behaviors, they can be experimented upon directly. When this is done, these verbal behaviors not only reveal orderliness with respect to both discriminative and reinforcing stimuli like that of nonverbal behaviors, but also they show their function as discriminative stimuli in directing and controlling other behaviors. In this, they show properties that they do not share with simpler motor activities, or with nonsense-syllables. A further, fuller empirical investigation of their quantitative characteristics should, we can state with some confidence, make questions of "awareness" of limited empirical significance. When these relationships are more fully elucidated, the word "awareness" may prove as dispensable as, say, phlogiston.

As an experimental strategy, then, let us remain unaware of awareness, but let us diligently ask the subject what he is or "thinks" he is, doing, and let us, using the methodology that has proven fruitful in showing the order in explicitly nonverbal behaviors, determine how such verbal statements behave, and, in turn, how they are related to—sometimes control—other ongoing activities.

Summary

A series of experiments has been summarized, in historical rather than logical order. The results of these experiments indicate that one type of verbal operant, the *notate,* a discriminated verbal response by a subject to stimuli experimentally presented, occurs in at least four kinds of situations, "concept-identification," "problem-solving," "association," and "conditioning." In two of these it becomes chained with other such operants, to form the *notant*—a fuller verbal statement about the environment, or the *monent*—a self-administered instruction, that is, an S^D for further behavior. All three classes of operant, each behaving slightly differently from one another, seem to constitute the behavioral basis of statements about "hypotheses." Unlike "mediating responses," or "processes," these verbal behaviors are not theoretically inferred, or indirectly manipulated, but rather are subject to direct experimental investigation. The relationship of their strength to the strength of the behaviors that they control is demonstrable.

References

Bousfield, W. A., & Cohen, B. H.   The effect of reinforcement on the occurrence of clustering in the recall of randomly arranged words of different frequencies of usage. *J. gen. Psychol.,* 1953, 52, 83-95.

Estes, W. K.   Effects of competing reactions on the conditioning curve for bar pressing. *J. exp. Psychol.,* 1950, 40, 200-205.

Gibson, J. J.   The concept of the stimulus in psychology. *Amer. Psychologist,* 1960, 15, 694-703.

Grant, D. A.   The verbal control of behavior. Presidential address, Div. 3, read at APA, New York, September, 1961.

Green, E. J. Concept formation: A problem in human operant conditioning. *J. exp. Psychol.,* 1955, 49, 175-180.

Oskamp, S. Partial reinforcement in concept formation: "Hypotheses" in human learning. Unpublished Master's thesis, Stanford Univer., 1956.

Rilling, M. Acquisition and partial reinforcement of a concept under different verbal reinforcement conditions. Unpublished Master's thesis, Univer. of Maryland, 1962.

Shepard, R. N., Hovland, C. I., & Jenkins, H. M. Learning and memorization of classifications. *Psychol. Monogr.,* 1961, 75, No. 13 (Whole No. 517).

Skinner, B. F. *Verbal behavior.* New York: Appleton-Century-Crofts, 1957.

Underwood, B. J. Studies of distributed practice: XV. Verbal concept learning as a function of intralist interference. *J. exp. Psychol.,* 1957, 54, 33-40.

Verplanck, W. S. Burrhus F. Skinner. In W. K. Estes *et al., Modern learning theory.* New York: Appleton-Century-Crofts, 1954. Pp. 267-316.

Verplanck, W. S. The operant conditioning of human motor behavior. *Psychol. Bull.,* 1956, 53, 70-83.

Verplanck, W. S. A glossary of some terms used in the objective science of behavior. *Psychol. Rev.,* 1957, 64 (Suppl.), 1-42.

81
83
86
88